BR
Hot

BRAD PITT
Hot and Sexy

by
GRACE CATALANO

BANTAM BOOKS

NEW YORK • TORONTO • LONDON • SYDNEY • AUCKLAND

BRAD PITT: HOT AND SEXY

A Bantam Book/July 1995

ISBN: 0-553-57015-3

Published simultaneously in the United States and Canada

Bantam Books are published by Bantam Books, a division of Bantam
Doubleday Dell Publishing Group, Inc. Its trademark, consisting of
the words "Bantam Books" and the portrayal of a rooster, is Regis-
tered in U.S. Patent and Trademark Office and in other countries.
Marca Registrada. Bantam Books, 1540 Broadway, New York, New
York 10036.

PRINTED IN THE UNITED STATES OF AMERICA

OPM   0 9 8 7 6 5 4 3 2 1

*To Joseph, for always thinking
the same thing I am.
You're the best!*

CONTENTS

ACKNOWLEDGMENTS

The author would like to thank Mary Michaels, Sam Alan, Grace Palazzo, Ralph J. Miele and Jane Burns.

Also, special thanks to Beverly Horowitz, Kathy Squires, Ellen Titlebaum, and everyone who worked on this book at Bantam Doubleday Dell.

And all my love to my parents, Rosemarie and Salvatore, who continue to support me!

one

Mad for Brad

Brad Pitt is sizzling hot! He's the sexiest guy on the big screen and the best new actor to emerge in a long time. He's not only gorgeous, he is also sensitive and alluring. With Robert Redford looks and James Dean talent, Brad is so much in demand that his asking price, according to *People* magazine, is somewhere near $7 million a picture.

Yet Brad Pitt insists he became a superstar unintentionally: He really only wanted to be a good actor who worked steadily. But Brad has become one of the world's brightest stars because of his extraordinary performances in movies like *A River Runs Through It, Interview With the Vampire* and *Legends of the Fall*.

Brad's acting has been universally showered with praise. A highlight of his career was receiving a 1994 Golden Globe nomination as Best

Actor for his electrifying portrayal of the reckless Tristan in *Legends of the Fall*.

An incredible drive for success is a big part of Brad's amazing life story. Born and raised in the American heartland, he's a country boy who hails from the Ozarks and speaks in a Missouri drawl. He stayed in Missouri until just two weeks before he would have graduated from the University of Missouri. Then he decided to head to California to pursue a career in the arts. With only $325 in his pocket and a head full of dreams, he was determined to survive by working odd jobs and going to as many auditions as he could.

The path Brad has traveled to fame and fortune has not always been smooth. He's earned his stardom the old-fashioned way: by working up the ladder of success one step at a time. He went from an unknown, struggling actor to a well-respected star. Finally he took Hollywood by storm. It didn't happen overnight. Brad has clearly paid his dues.

What was it that turned a handsome, talented boy from Missouri into the hottest star in Hollywood? The life and career of Brad Pitt make an American success story, filled with highs and lows, triumphs and disappointments. He is a largely self-taught actor who has become a superstar by relying almost exclusively on his own judgment.

People who have worked with Brad gush over him. David Geffen, who produced *Interview With the Vampire,* said, "Brad is one of the most attractive and talented men in the world today. He's going to be one of the biggest actors out there." When Brad appeared on the cover of *Rolling Stone* in December '94, that issue of the magazine became the second-best-selling one of the year.

The month of January 1995 belonged to Brad Pitt. His movie *Legends of the Fall* was number one at the box office for four weeks in a row, earning more than $65 million. His gorgeous face graced the covers of *Vanity Fair* and *People* in the same week. While *Vanity Fair* called him "Hollywood's Ultimate Sex Symbol," *People* gave him its highest honor, naming him "The Sexiest Man Alive."

Brad Pitt mania is reaching record proportions, and his millions of fans want to know everything about him. Where did Brad come from? Who is he dating? How does he feel about his newfound fame? What are his plans?

Perhaps the secret of Brad's success is that there's a lot of him in all his roles.

"The giant step of my career was *Thelma &*

Louise," said Brad. "I figured it would be a role like J.D.—something I'm good at, a Southern guy—that would make the break. It basically opened the door for some kind of respect."

And now that the door is wide open for Brad Pitt, it doesn't look as if it's going to close anytime soon!

two

Hero of the Heartland

The oldest of three children, William Bradley Pitt was born on December 18, 1963, in Shawnee, Oklahoma, but grew up in the city of Springfield, Missouri. From the beginning his family chose to call him Brad to distinguish him from his father, after whom he was named.

Bill Pitt worked his way up to an executive position in a trucking company. Brad always looked up to his father, though he thought he worked too hard. While Brad was growing up, Bill was often on the road. He would make up the lost time with his kids by taking them on his trips when they were on vacation from school. But even though Brad inherited Bill's love of the open road, he still doesn't understand why his dad had to be away from the family so much. "My father spent thirty-six years, six days a week on the job," Brad said. "But *we* never saw the sun."

More than anyone else in young Brad's life, his father and mother were his guides. Brad has said his mother was the first person who told him he was talented. "She just thought it from day one," he explained.

Jane Pitt, a school counselor, has described her family as "very close-knit." Chris Schudy, one of Brad's college friends, said, "Brad looks like his father, and he has the personality of his mother. His mother is so down-to-earth, just a super woman. His dad is a great guy but more reserved. *A River Runs Through It* is almost a mirror image of Brad's family. When I saw that movie, I called him and said, 'You're not even acting. It's just your home unit minus Julie.' "

Brad got along famously with his younger siblings, Doug and Julie. "I always looked up to both of my brothers," said Julie, the youngest of the Pitt children. "I just thought they were the greatest things that ever happened. Brad and Doug really play off each other. We just had such a close family, and that gave us confidence. I think that's what allowed Brad to try to be an actor. Sometimes I can't believe that this guy from Springfield made it, but Brad has always succeeded in everything he's done, and he's always had a way with people."

At the age of six Brad was already a head-turner as he performed in the choir at South Haven Baptist Church. He was a gorgeous child with a blond bowl haircut and crystal-clear blue eyes. Connie Bilyeu, the church's piano accompanist and later Brad's high-school drama coach, said of him, "You couldn't keep from watching Brad because his face was so expressive. As he sang in the choir, he would move his little mouth so big with all the words that he attracted everyone's attention."

It was during his preteen years that Brad was introduced to music and movies, both of which became lifelong passions. For a while the only music he heard was the songs he sang in church; he didn't know the effect music could have on him until the day he first heard Elton John's song "Daniel." He saved up his allowance to buy the *Captain Fantastic* album and played it constantly. Elton John soon became Brad's favorite singer; Brad would even quote lines from his songs.

Brad collected all of Elton John's albums in the 1970s, but John wasn't the only singer Brad listened to. Another favorite album was The Who's *Tommy*. When the movie version, which

7

starred not only Roger Daltrey of The Who, but also Elton John, was released in 1975, Brad went to see it twice because he loved Elton's Pinball Wizard part.

Brad found escape in movies; they introduced him to aspects of life he knew little about. His taste in film ranged from tearjerkers to science fiction. Among his other favorites were *Ordinary People* and *Saturday Night Fever*.

The one film that left the biggest impression on young Brad was the futuristic thriller *Planet of the Apes*. He went to see it with his parents at the drive-in, and it really stuck with him. Sitting on the hood of the family car, Brad ate a bucket of popcorn and was amazed at the imagination of the filmmakers. He still says the final scene, in which Charlton Heston sees the Statue of Liberty buried in the sand, is one of the greatest movie moments of all time.

For the most part, Brad's early years were extremely happy. His parents raised their children to go after their dreams, to do something they enjoyed. Bill encouraged individuality in his young son, and his encouragement would eventually pay off.

As Brad grew older, he developed an enthusiastic spirit and a taste for adventure. In high school he got involved in student government, debating, sports, plays, and madrigal singing. Sandra Grey Wagner, who was the assistant principal of Kickapoo High School during Brad's years there in the early 1980s, said she remembers him as "a super kid."

Brad pushed himself into trying everything. And when he attempted something, he went all the way. Naturally athletic, he enjoyed sports, but tennis, he soon found out, was not at the top of his list. Still, once he signed up for tennis, he stayed with it until he was competing in tournaments. He didn't *want* to compete, but he didn't know how to tell his parents.

When Bill Pitt once saw Brad on the court screaming and throwing his racket, he wisely gave his son some advice. "Between games, he just said, 'Are you having fun?' " Brad remembered. "I got all huffy and said, 'No.' And he looked at me and said, 'Then don't do it,' and then walked away. That put me in my place."

Brad's early years were much like those of many other American kids. He owned a BB gun. He loved to go camping. When he got his driver's license, his parents gave him their Buick Centurion 455, which Brad said "was passable because it was a two-door." Later he bought himself a used Nissan 200 SX, which he named Runaround Sun. He found most of his classes at school extremely boring but was a good student. He has a couple of scars on his face that he got as a kid playing sports. One scar across his cheekbone comes from an injury he suffered while playing baseball. "It was a pop fly that I lost in the sun. I still threw the guy out on second after it dropped on my face."

Brad was far from a tough kid in school, but he did stand up for what he thought was right, and sometimes that included getting into fights with other kids. "It's really easy to get out of a fight," he said. "But when you're a kid, you just swing and ask questions later." Often he got in trouble sticking up for friends.

Brad had a lot of friends in school; some he keeps in contact with. He loved girls and started dating during junior high school. "I was always completely intrigued, taken over, would do anything for girls," he said. He had discovered women in elementary school, when he and some friends found a stack of *Playboy* magazines in a house being built. "I was very impressed," he said. "I was just so *overwhelmed*."

By the seventh grade Brad was already extremely popular with girls; they loved him not only because he was the best-looking kid in Springfield, but because he was so much fun to be around.

Young Brad played host at a lot of parties in his parents' basement. It was finished and set up with a TV, a sofa and a couple of beanbag chairs. Brad's parents allowed the parties, but he says his mother was always checking up on him and the other kids.

"My mom always made a lot of noise before opening the door to the basement. She'd call down, 'Brad? Can I come down and get something out of the freezer?' Of course, you had to wonder why Mom needed a frozen steak at ten o'clock at night."

Brad's parties usually involved music, dancing and a lot of kissing. He says the girls he dated all through high school "usually overdid it with that flavored lip gloss. But we didn't know it at the time. We thought it was fine!"

As a senior in high school Brad began dating Sarah Hart, who became his last, and probably most serious, girlfriend before he went off to college. When Brad's debate team had a tournament with the other high school in town, Sarah was on the other team. Their meeting took place in a school hallway. Ever the romantic, Brad was immediately smitten with dark-haired Sarah and, with his usual charm, began to pursue her.

Sarah remembered that Brad sent her a note while she was in class one day. It said, "Look in

11

the snow, there'll be a surprise for you." When Sarah looked out the window, Brad and a friend were running back and forth, writing out her name in the snow with their feet.

Next Brad sent her another note; this time she received it during choir practice. The choir was abuzz as everyone asked her what was in the note; when she opened it, she read that Brad was asking her out. To this day Sarah has the note. Brad had written that he thought it was important for them to get together because it would be good public relations between their schools. He gave Sarah his telephone number and asked her whether she wanted to go out Saturday or Sunday. "I called him and told him I'd like to go out on Saturday," Sarah remembered. "He said, 'That's Valentine's Day.' It seemed very romantic to have our first date on Valentine's Day."

Normally Brad liked to take girls out to the movies, and that was often where he and Sarah ended up. But that first time was different. Brad decided to take Sarah to a restaurant, then home to meet his family. They ended the evening by watching TV in the Pitts' basement. Brad's sister, Julie, who was then in junior high, kept checking on them, giggling and asking if they were kissing.

Brad dated Sarah until he graduated from high school. Since their proms were on the same night, they went to both of them, but their relationship didn't last much longer. Sarah said they had some fun times and some fights. After one fight Brad sent her a dozen roses with a nasty note inside. He was angry because she hadn't called him all week and told her so in the note. That was the beginning of the end of their relationship.

The last time Sarah saw Brad was the day they officially broke up. They had plans to go out, but Brad stood Sarah up and went to play miniature golf with his friends instead. The next day Sarah saw him for the last time in his driveway. "He was very much into Elton John and quoted the words to 'Sorry Seems to Be the Hardest Word,' " said Sarah. "When we broke up, we were both going to college anyway."

College was a terrific experience for Brad. He left home to attend the University of Missouri at Columbia, where he majored in journalism, though he was interested in becoming an advertising art director. At the age of seventeen, he had started to take a real interest in art. He can often be spotted in art museums and galleries today.

"It was about creating, creating a successful, imaginative ad campaign that interested me," said Brad, explaining why he wanted to go into advertising. Later his ideas changed, but he was quick to point out, "I'm not knocking the job.

It's an individual thing. I just realized there was something better."

Brad thoroughly enjoyed his college days. He was a member of Sigma Chi fraternity and often posed shirtless for campus calendars printed to raise funds. College opened up a whole new world for Brad; he made a bunch of friends, including Chris Schudy, who remains a close pal. When Brad speaks about his college days, he has great things to say. "It was incredible just to get away from home, living with a bunch of guys," he said. "We had this idea of *Animal House,* and there was definitely that aspect. It was a highlight, without a doubt. Then, like everything else, you grow out of it."

In 1986, right before graduation, Brad had a change of heart. He no longer wanted to go into advertising, because his teachers "were doggin' all my ideas. They wanted the straight thing and it was really boring." Brad abruptly decided that the best thing to do was leave college and home to search for the work that truly interested him.

"You keep finding things in little increments," he said. "Each one of those little increments led me to saying, 'I don't want to do this. I want to go over there and see what that's all about. I had a great time in college. I learned more about being on my own than anything from a book. It's just as important to find what you don't want to do as what you want to do."

What Brad wanted to do was set out for California. "I decided everyone was applying for a job or getting married," he said, "and I didn't want to do either."

When he told his parents he was leaving school, he quickly informed them he was going to enroll in the Art Center College of Design in Pasadena. He was considering the idea but never pursued it.

Once Brad had the idea of leaving his home state, he became very excited. "You don't really get it into your head that you can leave," he said. "Not too many people leave. Till it was about time to graduate and it just dawned on me, 'I can leave.' It would be simple, so easy. You load up the car, you point it west, and you leave."

Thinking back on his decision, Brad said, "It was such a relief. I was coming to the end of college and the end of my degree and the beginning of my chosen occupation. I knew I didn't want to do it."

He dreamed of pursuing a career in music. He saw himself as a rock star, but had no idea where to begin. He also enjoyed acting; he had appeared in high-school plays and fraternity shows.

Suddenly he was wondering which road to

15

take. After thinking about it, Brad put his plan into action. Just two weeks before graduation and two credits shy of getting his degree in journalism, Brad abandoned college and his prospects in advertising for the adventure of going to California. He packed his bags and—not telling his parents the truth—headed for Hollywood with $325 in his pocket. He was determined to show the world what Brad Pitt had to offer.

three

Surviving in Hollywood

Traveling west to California was the logical next step for a youth as unsettled as Brad, who had to grow in many ways before his talents could take hold. "I always knew I'd leave Missouri," Brad has said. "But it's like that Tom Waits song, 'I never saw my hometown until I stayed away too long.' I love my hometown. I just wanted to see more. You'd come across a book or something on TV, and you'd see all these other worlds. It blew me away."

Brad could easily have settled down and gotten himself a "real" job after college, but he chose to do the opposite; he chose to shake things up, possibly to study art in new surroundings, to see the world—alone. He needed to get away from Missouri, away from friends and family, and see what else was out there. Just driving from Missouri to California gave him a sense of adventure he had never felt before. "I remember being so excited as I passed each state line," he said. "I drove in through Burbank, and the smog was so thick that it seemed like fog. I pulled in and went to McDonald's, and that was it. I just thought, 'Shouldn't there be a little more?' "

Hollywood had been a magnet for thousands of young people who wanted to get into a business they knew nothing about. Once Brad hit Hollywood, he was faced with the insecurity of "not knowing." He didn't know how he would go about breaking into acting or music, nor did he know the two most important things: where he would live and what he would live on when his $325 ran out. For some reason, none of this bothered him.

He tackled his days one at a time. He rented a tiny West Hollywood apartment, sharing it with a roommate, and set out to find work. Going to art school became the furthest thing from his mind. Instead he focused on his dreams: music first, and then acting. He was leaning more toward becoming a rock star than toward becoming a movie star. He often played guitar in jam sessions with local musician friends. But as he soon found out, music was not the route for him.

Brad also learned how fast $325 could slip

through his fingers. Too proud to borrow from his parents, he took any job he could find. He delivered refrigerators to college students, collected money for a police ball, passed out cigarette samples, chauffeured a limousine for a strip-o-gram service and got into a giant chicken suit for the fast-food restaurant El Pollo Loco. This last was the closest thing to an acting job he could get. He stood outside El Pollo Loco waving at the cars going by, trying to lure customers in to buy chicken. He would later describe this job as very embarrassing. "I'd stand on the corner of Sunset Boulevard in hundred-degree weather and flap my wings in front of the place," he said in an interview in 1988.

Brad was living the classic life of a struggling actor, but he didn't see it that way. "At the time, it was all exciting," he said, "though I wouldn't want to go back and do it now." Looking back on this period, Brad said the experience was valuable not only because it toughened his professional skin but because it gave him a unique perspective on life. "L.A. and Missouri are like the North and South Poles—they're a world apart. But each one is good in a different way. Back home I was close to lakes and hills, and I missed that, but when I first moved to L.A., it was a real adventure."

Anyone living in or visiting California can feel the thrill of the movies in the air. The film trade magazines are on sale at every roadside, along with phony maps of the stars' homes. Casual talk in stores inevitably turns to movies, and well-known and lesser-known faces from the big screen are often seen in corner shops and restaurants. After working a series of odd jobs, Brad began to consider seriously a career in acting. He was often told by people he met that he should be in the movies, that he had the look talent agents were searching for. But it took him a while before he figured out how to break into acting.

His world started to change one day when a woman he was chauffeuring referred him to the acting coach Roy London. London was a highly respected teacher in town; he taught many stars their craft, among them Michelle Pfeiffer and Sharon Stone. Brad jumped at the chance to study acting with London. Finally, he thought, there was hope that he could become a working actor.

It was the late eighties, and a new wave of twentysomething actors was beginning to make it big in Hollywood. The word was that agents and managers were eagerly looking for new young stars, and Brad was ready.

From the beginning of his studies, it was clear

that Brad wasn't stamped from the ordinary actor's mold. He read lines with the conviction and skill of an actor twice his age. His acting style attracted the attention of many agents. There were always agents hanging around acting classes, hoping to sign new talent.

Brad was officially "discovered" by one of these agents, in a way he has described as "cliché." A young woman in his acting class was going to audition for a big agency, and she asked Brad if he would be her scene partner for the audition. He said yes; they did the scene, and the agency signed Brad and passed on his friend.

At first Brad couldn't understand why he needed to be represented. Knowing practically nothing about show business, he didn't realize that an agent would be able to get him into closed auditions. Still, he signed and waited. He knew he'd done the right thing, but the rewards were very small at first.

When he got a job as an extra in the movie *Less Than Zero* (released in 1987) and the jobs seemed to be coming in at a slow but steady pace, he decided to call home with the news. He hadn't yet told his parents that he was pursuing an acting career. They were still under the impression that he was out in California studying art and getting ready for a career in advertising. The reason he didn't spill the beans to them was simply that he didn't want them to worry unnecessarily. He called home three times a week because, he said, his mother would've been mad at him if he didn't phone. But he didn't tell them about his array of jobs or that he was trying to be an actor. When he finally revealed the truth, they weren't completely surprised.

His father's answer was "Yeah, I thought so." His mother later said, "Brad is someone who's always liked to try new things. No one was surprised."

But the news did surprise his classmates and friends back home. After all, they didn't know him as well as his family did. Chris Schudy, Brad's college friend, said, "People at Missouri were really surprised when they found out what Brad was doing. But he's always been so charming that it made some sense. The first time my mom met him, she called him a little Roman god."

The news that Brad had hit the big time in Hollywood spread all over his hometown. He was the talk of Springfield; he still is today. His success even inspired four of his friends to drop what they were doing and move out to Hollywood to try their luck at acting. They figured that if

Brad could do it, so could they. But it wasn't that easy.

At first it wasn't easy for Brad, either, though he had looks and talent. It took a while before he started to receive the rave reviews he gets today. While he was waiting for his big break, Brad continued to work odd jobs. He was finding the jobs increasingly difficult to hold because he tried to get to every audition he could.

The first anniversary of his move to California came and went, and he felt that he hadn't moved one step up the ladder of success. He spent all the money he earned on rent and Taco Bell burritos. His acting career might be off to a good start, but he still hadn't won a decent role.

four
Drifting into Acting

Brad began his acting career by playing a diverse group of characters on television. In the beginning the parts he got were very small. The movie *Less Than Zero,* which starred Andrew McCarthy and Robert Downey, Jr., gave Brad his first experience on a movie set. As an extra, Brad had no lines and appeared in an if-you-blink-you'll-miss-him scene, but he was happy to be hanging around the cameras, crew and other actors. After *Less Than Zero* Brad nabbed a short-lived role in the daytime drama *Another World*. This part sent Brad on his maiden voyage to New York City.

Brad found the trip to New York more interesting than his role on the soap. He found Manhattan exhilarating. On days when he wasn't working at the television studio, he took a bite out of the Big Apple by trying to see some of the city's most famous sights. He especially enjoyed walking through the museums and galleries. But just as he was beginning to get used to life in Manhattan, he was written out of *Another World* and on his way back to California.

Brad was back to square one and began the long and arduous procedure of auditioning. This part of acting has never been Brad's favorite. He found auditions too competitive and, at first, very intimidating. While they're part of the business, trying out for roles and getting rejected can be the most grueling things an aspiring actor has to do. This excruciating process can definitely take its toll on a young, enthusiastic future star. Brad was no exception, though he won most of the parts he went out for. Sitting in a room with actors all vying for the same role was so difficult for him, he decided that the only way to get through them was not to talk to anyone but the casting directors. He would walk in and study the script; he found that he did better if he gave himself the opportunity to concentrate on the character he was trying out for.

Brad's agents sent him on calls for nearly every TV show that needed a young male actor. He was also sent to auditions for commercials. They were work, and they paid the rent. Not only that, but commercials were a great training ground.

Learning how to work for eight hours on a set is the best way to get used to the acting business. Plunging into commercials full-time, Brad appeared in spots for Levi's jeans and Mountain Dew soda. His appearance in a sexy Levi's TV ad ultimately brought him his first taste of national attention.

In 1987 Brad went to read for a new character on the TV series *Our House*. The family drama filled a popular slot in the Sunday-night lineup. It starred character actor Wilford Brimley, teen idol Chad Allen and the then unknown, fifteen-year-old Shannen Doherty, who later gained fame on *Beverly Hills 90210*.

Brad was there to read for a character who was going to be written into the show. But instead of being cast on *Our House,* he was sent to the studio next door to read for the producers of *Dallas*. They were also casting a new character, and Brad was in the right place at the right time. He felt good at the audition, and by that afternoon he got the call telling him he'd been cast as Randy, the boyfriend of Charlie Wade, played by Shalane McCall. As for his audition for *Our House*, he found out later that the producers had dropped their plans to add the character to the show.

Brad felt it had all worked out for the best; he

thought *Dallas* would be a better career move. Having hit the airwaves in 1978, *Dallas* was the most popular series on the air throughout the 1980s. It was the first successful nighttime soap opera since *Peyton Place* in the late 1960s, and it was the first series to bring back the cliffhanger ending of the final episode in each season. These cliffhangers were designed to keep audiences in suspense throughout five months of reruns during the late spring and summer. The most famous cliffhanger in the history of *Dallas* closed the 1979–80 season; at the end of the final episode, J.R. (played by Larry Hagman) was shot in the chest by an unknown assailant. The episode generated months of worldwide publicity; everyone tried to figure out the answer to that year's most-asked question: "Who shot J.R.?" When it was finally answered, on November 21, 1980, that episode became one of the most widely watched TV shows of all time. The success of *Dallas* spawned a host of imitators during the 1980s; three or four prime-time serials hit the airwaves every season, but only a few stayed on the air, among them *Dynasty* and the *Dallas* spinoff *Knots Landing*.

By the time Brad got to *Dallas* in 1987, the show wasn't quite the success it had been. A whole new crop of characters had been introduced, and the hype surrounding the hourlong drama was diminishing.

The role Brad played was in the Priscilla Presley story line. Priscilla, who played Jenna Wade, had joined *Dallas* in 1983. That same year, a pretty ten-year-old actress named Shalane McCall was cast as her daughter, Charlie. As the years rolled by, Shalane blossomed into a beautiful teenager, and the producers thought it was time to give her a story line. On the show she had gone from a sweet, naive girl to a rebel. Her best story line included her relationship with Brad's character; Shalane believed the producers and writers were finally giving her an interesting part to play.

Unfortunately, just as things got rolling for Shalane and Brad, it all came to a screeching halt. Priscilla Presley went off the show after the 1987 season and her entire story line went with her, including Brad and Shalane.

Looking back on the five episodes he appeared in, Brad referred to his character as "an idiot boyfriend who gets caught in the hay." But at the time he was excited about winning the role and being on TV for five weeks straight. *Dallas* was Brad's first "real job" as an actor. He began to be recognized in public; he received fan mail, and teen magazines expressed interest in doing feature stories on him.

Up to then Brad had had a tough time getting coverage in magazines, but suddenly he was deluged with requests for interviews and photographs. He also heard the first questions about his personal life. What kind of girl did he like? Was he dating anyone special?

The answer was that Brad found himself too wrapped up in his career for a serious emotional involvement. If he wanted a girlfriend, he didn't have to look very far. Actresses, extras, and secretaries were constantly buzzing around him.

The nearest thing to a steady girlfriend was Shalane McCall, his *Dallas* costar. From the first day they met on the set, they seemed to feel an attraction. The first scene they appeared in together involved them in a passionate kiss. On TV productions, actors are usually shuffled around the set, and *Dallas* was no different. Brad had met Shalane only briefly before he found himself kissing her while the cameras rolled. They hadn't had a chance to say more than a few words to each other, but they soon became fast friends.

Shalane had been in show business most of her young life. When Brad met her, she had already been on *Dallas* for five seasons. She had accumulated an armful of trophies, including two Soap Opera awards, a Youth-in-Film award and a Rising Star award. There was an eight-year age difference between Brad and Shalane, but that didn't stop them from having an offscreen relationship.

Though at the time they admitted to being just good friends, Brad saw Shalane romantically for two months. They posed for countless photos together, went to parties, and became the talk of Hollywood. But their romance didn't last beyond *Dallas*. Brad couldn't tie himself down in any kind of relationship; he had to get his career going at full speed before he could even think about settling down.

Saying goodbye to Shalane was difficult for Brad. Shalane was equally upset; she cared for Brad a great deal. But they both thought it was for the best. Shalane later began dating Frank Zappa's son Ahmet regularly, while Brad concentrated on his career.

Appearing on *Dallas* opened a lot of doors for Brad. He turned up in teen magazines regularly and was becoming a hot heartthrob. But his coverage was cut short when his *Dallas* days ended. He had enjoyed his moment in the spotlight and was sad to see it end so quickly. But he tried not to let it bother him too much. The kind of fame

Kirk Cameron and River Phoenix had found at the time eluded Brad, but being in Hollywood did have one advantage: He kept working.

Thanks to his credentials, slim as they were, Brad managed to get himself a guest-starring role on the highly successful sitcom *Growing Pains,* the show that turned Kirk Cameron into a star. Outgoing, clean-cut Brad played a bad-boy transfer student who almost steals the heart of Carol Seaver (played by Tracey Gold). The entire half hour revolved around Brad's character.

When he appeared on *Growing Pains,* it was at the height of its success. Kirk Cameron, the show's star, was a teen idol who filmed movies when he was on hiatus from the show. Brad was very impressed with Kirk and expressed his opinions about him right after he filmed the episode: "I think someone in that position, who's looked up to that much and has that much money and power at that age, could really get messed up. I've seen some of it out here. Kirk is just completely humble. I learned how I would want to be if things ever got rolling for me."

After *Growing Pains,* Brad played another bad-boy character on an episode of *21 Jump Street,* which launched the careers of two other teen idols, Johnny Depp and Richard Grieco. Producer Patrick Hasburgh cast Brad in that episode because he spotted something special in the young actor. "Even at that time, Brad walking into a room was more exciting than most actors doing a scene," said Hasburgh later.

In 1988, far from being the golden boy of the entertainment industry that he is today, Brad was still not much more than a small-time TV star. But he believed he had come a long way and considered himself lucky beyond his wildest dreams. After all, he was just a kid from a small town who'd come to Hollywood with no experience and no contacts. He'd done a pretty good job of getting himself noticed. But even he knew that it wasn't enough.

Brad wanted more: He wanted to do a movie, a real movie that would be shown on a big screen in a theater. He even considered doing made-for-TV movies, as long as he could play interesting characters. Brad knew he had to knock on more doors and get himself into a good role. He had to play the waiting game a little longer.

five

Reaching for Stardom

Brad Pitt disagreed with his agents. They wanted to keep him tied to television, hoping to turn him into the next big TV star. But Brad had bigger dreams. He set his sights on the movies, where he believed an actor could have professional freedom. He didn't like working within the confines of a television series, especially a sitcom. To Brad, film was the one place where a character could be developed completely, from beginning to end.

Unfortunately for Brad, what he dreamed of doing and what was being offered to him were two different things. He was in no position yet to be choosy; he took any role he could get, even if it was on the small screen. More guest appearances came from every direction. One week Brad was on sitcoms like *Head of the Class* and *Trial and Error;* the next he was doing serious drama on the critically acclaimed *Thirtysomething*.

When a movie finally did come along, it came in the form of a teen comedy-horror film titled *Cutting Class*. While landing a starring role in the film was lucky for him, it wasn't *that* lucky. According to Brad, *Cutting Class* is the worst movie he ever did.

"I spend all my time, until like four in the morning, watching bad movies," he said, grinning. "Richard Grieco did this one that is just the best. It's called *Tomcat: Dangerous Desires*. That's 'Tomcat, colon, Dangerous Desires.' Wow." As his grin turned into a laugh, Brad continued, "I was in one myself, and by all means, please seek it out. It's called *Cutting Class*. Just awful."

Cutting Class is a dark comedy spoofing teenage slasher films like *Nightmare on Elm Street* and *Friday the 13th*. Brad, as good guy Dwight Ingalls, was the third star of the film, behind Jill Schoelen (best known for *The Stepfather*), who played his girlfriend, Paula Carson, and the top-billed star Donovan Leitch (son of the singer Donovan) as the film's maniac killer, Brian Woods. *Cutting Class,* which costarred veteran actor Roddy McDowall and comedian Martin Mull, received pretty bad reviews when it hit

34

theaters in 1989. One critic wrote, "Brad Pitt and Jill Schoelen are both appealing even in this dunce-cap comedy." It was a complete bomb at the box office, opening and disappearing from theaters within a few weeks.

On the positive side, Brad and Jill became very close after filming on *Cutting Class* had wrapped. They dated for a couple of months, but their work took them in different directions.

Brad's next feature film was another disaster. It was *Happy Together,* released in 1990, an incredibly low-budget movie starring Patrick Dempsey, Helen Slater and Dan Schneider (of *Head of the Class*). Brad probably shouldn't have even bothered to take this role, but he chalked it up to experience and temporarily added it to his résumé.

He was disillusioned with the parts he was getting on the big screen, and he next decided to accept two roles on TV. One was a small part in HBO's *The Image,* which boasted a cast of fine actors: Albert Finney, Kathy Baker, John Mahoney and Swoosie Kurtz.

The other role changed Brad's life. His first really prominent part came in the TV movie *Too Young to Die?,* a fact-inspired drama that starred Juliette Lewis as Amanda, a fifteen-year-old girl faced with the death penalty after committing a brutal murder. The movie asked the question: When is someone old enough to receive a death sentence? As Billy, the small-time hood who leads Amanda down her path of destruction, Brad was chillingly believable.

The TV movie proved to be a landmark in the young life and career of Brad Pitt. Not only did his performance bring him to the forefront of the entertainment business, it also introduced him to the film's star, Juliette Lewis, an actress who became a big part of Brad's life offscreen.

Too Young to Die? showed the powerful performances both Brad and Juliette were capable of. One reviewer wrote, "The cast is first-rate! Lewis invests her hard-eyed, tough-talking Amanda with a fundamental innocence and pain. Lewis gives her character a dignity that a supposed throwaway like Amanda is rarely granted on TV." In the same review, Brad's performance was also singled out: "Pitt is a magnificent slime-ball as Amanda's hoody boyfriend; looking and sounding like a malevolent John Cougar Mellencamp, he's really scary."

Finally Brad had been given the chance to show his talent. He fell into the role, playing it to perfection. In fact, he did such a magnificent job that it shocked his whole family when they saw it on the evening of February 26, 1990.

It was the first time his parents really got to see Brad develop a character. He said, "I think my whole family were blown away by what I did in that film."

While it seemed as if Brad was finally on a professional winning streak, he next made an unfortunate choice, taking a role in a new Fox TV series, *Glory Days*. Because of the success of *Beverly Hills 90210*, Fox tried several times to duplicate that series' premise, creating other shows starring an ensemble cast of young, hip, good-looking actors. Fox found out that this concept didn't work every time.

Glory Days debuted on Fox on July 25, 1990, and lasted only until September 27, 1990—just six episodes. The hourlong drama revolved around the lives of four best friends. It starred Spike Alexander as Dave Rutecki, a rookie cop; Evan Mirand as Fopiano, a fraternity pledge; Nicholas Kalls as Peter "T-Bone" Trigg, a rock-and-roll fan; and Brad as Walker Lovejoy, a college dropout and aspiring newspaper writer.

Looking back on the series, Brad called it "terrible. I'd rather do nothing than to get involved in something like that again."

It was a lucky thing for Brad that *Glory Days* wasn't a runaway hit, because it would have stifled his movie career and taken him out of the running for major roles. No doubt the success of the series would have sent Brad in a whole new direction. Instead, freed from the series, Brad was once again showing up at auditions.

Almost immediately he was cast in *Across the Tracks,* a low-budget movie released in 1991 that starred former child star Rick Schroder. Of all Brad's early features, *Across the Tracks,* though it did not enjoy commercial success, was perhaps the best. The role Brad played gave him personal satisfaction, since he played one of two lead characters who carried the movie from beginning to end.

Across the Tracks was reviewed in few papers, but one critic wrote, "The film's strength lies in the two leads, particularly Brad Pitt's depiction of Joe, whose virtue and discipline mask an obsessed, fragile personality."

Other reviewers called Brad "a promising young male lead who could develop into a major player."

Before long Brad Pitt was taking his biggest acting chance yet, playing a sexy hitchhiker in a major motion picture called *Thelma & Louise.* It was the role that finally launched his career as a star.

six

Fifteen Minutes of Fame

Brad Pitt was not the first choice for the small but pivotal role of J.D. in the blockbuster movie *Thelma & Louise*. In fact, Brad wasn't even thought of until William Baldwin backed out at the last minute to star in Ron Howard's movie *Backdraft*. That decision left director Ridley Scott (*Alien, Blade Runner, Legend*) and casting director Lou DiGiaimo wondering if they would find the right actor for the important part.

Brad had been one of four hundred hopefuls who auditioned for the star-making role. And it was Brad who stuck out in Lou DiGiaimo's mind. "There are stars who aren't great actors," DiGiaimo said. "But when I met Brad, I thought, 'He's going to be a star *and* he can *act*.' His career is going to be capital B-I-G."

It was DiGiaimo who convinced Ridley Scott

39

that Brad should play J.D. Scott called Brad in for a second audition. This time he read a scene with Geena Davis, and the director was sold. Brad got the part, and three days later he was standing under a blazing-hot sun in the sands of Utah, ready to begin shooting.

Brad felt from the start that getting the role of J.D. "was meant to be." He craved the role, more than he had ever wanted anything else. It was, he thought, finally a step in the right direction. According to Brad, "I always figured my break would be playing a good ol' boy. I hear people gripe all the time about coming to L.A. and not being taken seriously. You have to show them. When I first started, I was being sent out on sitcoms. I like sitcoms, but I knew I wouldn't be good in them. So I have to find something I can do and go out and get it. Then they say, 'Oh, he can do that.'"

His role might not have been big and he might not have been paid very much, but neither of these facts mattered to Brad. What was most important to him was that he had nabbed an important part in a big-budget movie. The chance to work with a director like Ridley Scott and stars like Geena Davis and Susan Sarandon was more than he could have asked for.

Brad approached his new role with his usual

zest, setting out to prove that he was the right man for the job. His attitude that he should always strive "to be the best I can be" was apparent the minute he first went onscreen.

Neil Jordan, who later directed Brad in *Interview With the Vampire*, said of his star quality, "Brad has kind of come into acting by being himself, hasn't he? He's come into it by being this incredibly charismatic character. But I think he's far better than he pretends he thinks he is. I think he's great, and I think he actually knows he's great. People are either stars, or they're not. They either project it, or they don't. The minute Brad walked into *Thelma & Louise* he did that. He was a star from then on."

Before Brad filmed his role, he met with director Ridley Scott, who discussed his ideas with the young actor. Scott described the movie he wanted to make, the story he wanted to tell, and how important he believed Brad's role was to the story. Scott had complete faith in Brad and told him so, giving Brad total confidence. For Brad, working with such a respected director was an honor beyond words. He had long admired Scott's work.

Thelma & Louise is the story of two women who set out on a weekend camping trip and end up on a joyriding flight from the law. Their lives are changed when they interrupt their drive to stop at a country bar for some dancing and a good time. When Harlan (Timothy Carhart), one of the locals, attacks Thelma (Geena Davis) in the parking lot, Louise (Susan Sarandon) shoots and kills him. She then convinces Thelma that the police will not believe their story, and the two flee in panic.

Driving from Arkansas, they head through Oklahoma, where they pick up J.D. (Brad), a gorgeous cowboy hitching a ride. He spends a passionate night with Thelma, then steals the pair's $6,600.

With the FBI following them from one county to the other, Thelma and Louise become desperadoes, running from the law and robbing stores to finance their escape to Mexico. The film's final scene involves the FBI surrounding them in the middle of the desert. Agreeing to go out with a bang rather than surrender, Thelma and Louise speed their convertible over the edge of the Grand Canyon.

Brad's performance is perhaps the closest to his own personality, although he said with a laugh, "I don't go around robbing people."

The one part Brad was most nervous about filming was the love scene with Geena Davis. It took an entire day to get that scene on film the way Ridley Scott had envisioned it. One crew member said Brad was "skittish about doing the scene. His biggest worry was that his mother wouldn't approve. He was absolutely charming and very shy."

The long day's shoot was made easier by Geena Davis, who immediately calmed down her young costar. "She wouldn't *let* me be nervous," Brad said later. "Geena and Susan were both really cool. They made me feel very comfortable."

The love scene was very effective once it was completed, but it wasn't all that glamorous to film. "Let me tell you, it was really romantic for all thirty of us in the room," explained Brad wryly. "It's a long day when you're running around with a patch over your personals. We were all fighting over what music to play to break the tension. Geena wanted Prince and I wanted John Lee Hooker and some sexy blues—we played it all. It turned out to be a great day."

Right before *Thelma & Louise* hit the theaters, the Hollywood rumor mill churned out the story that Brad and Geena Davis were a new twosome. The media, hungry for any gossipy tidbit they could get to fill the tabloids, ate up the Brad-and-Geena story. But there was never any real foundation supporting this rumor. Though stories insinuated that Brad broke Geena's heart, the stars themselves denied ever being involved in a relationship offscreen. After all, except for their scenes in the movie, Brad and Geena had never been seen together in public.

The story didn't seem to bother Geena, Brad or the cast and crew; it was great advance publicity for the movie. It added fuel to the fire of *Thelma & Louise,* which was fast becoming one of the most talked-about pictures of the year. "This is a different kind of movie," Geena Davis said right before the film's release. "It's a movie about *women's adventures.*"

When *Thelma & Louise* opened in May 1991 it received rave reviews. Critics hailed this "female buddy film," calling it "fun" and "a highly enjoyable ride." Most critics were glad to see Ridley Scott abandon the dark sets of his past films for this exuberant road trip across a bright, glossy Western landscape. Geena Davis surprised many with her extraordinary performance as the ditzy Thelma, and Brad got great notices as the sexy scoundrel who had women of all ages swooning over him.

While girls and women everywhere started to take notice of Brad, the woman he was beginning to be seen around town with was Juliette Lewis. He took Juliette to the premiere of *Thelma &*

Louise, where it was obvious that the pair were seriously dating. Their romance had begun when they worked on the TV movie *Too Young to Die?*, but it intensified only months before Brad's big movie opened.

The first time Juliette and Brad spent time together was to do research for *Too Young to Die?*. "We got together to look at *The Panic in Needle Park* with Al Pacino for research, because we had to film our own drug scene for our movie," Juliette explained. "So we hung out in this hotel room in Taft, outside of L.A., watching the movie. I noticed that he had this black luggage, real organized. Matching. I had three different bags from all over. He had a CD case, I hadn't even moved up from tapes yet. He was organized to a certain extent, and that was really appealing to me. He was just really authentic. So then we drove back together—two hours of good, quality driving. We didn't say much. We listened to music. After that drive, we both knew we liked each other. We didn't even kiss. I was expecting it, because you move so fast these days. But he didn't; he gave me a hug. I tortured my best friend, Trish, over this for the next three weeks. Three weeks of 'What is he thinking?'!"

Brad was thinking the same thing as Juliette: They were immediately attracted to each other and wanted to get to know each other better. Juliette's background intrigued Brad. Juliette is a full-fledged showbiz kid who grew up on movie sets surrounded by actors. The daughter of actor Geoffrey Lewis (best known from the Clint Eastwood movies *Every Which Way but Loose* and *Any Which Way You Can*) and graphic designer Glenis Batley, Juliette was born on June 21, 1973.

At age twelve Juliette landed a role as the daughter in the Showtime miniseries *Homefires*. Like Brad, she spent a few years on TV doing sitcom work, or what she called "the sitcom curse. I played cheerleaders and airheads. Sitcoms demolish anyone of creativity."

The TV movie *Too Young to Die?* had the same positive effect on both Juliette and Brad. Their roles catapulted their careers to new heights. For Juliette, her big break was the role of Danielle in the 1991 Martin Scorsese thriller *Cape Fear*. She played that part so perfectly, it garnered her both Golden Globe and Academy Award nominations for Best Supporting Actress.

The young couple soon found themselves attending award shows and premieres. The media spotlight was now focused squarely on Brad; fans thrust pens and paper at him and photographers yelled for him to turn their way.

Though Juliette had grown up around Hollywood, she wasn't prepared for the fanfare Brad received the night of the *Thelma & Louise* premiere. "I don't have the kind of fame where people constantly scream around me," she said. "The first time I had a taste of that was when I went to Brad's premiere for *Thelma & Louise*. Everyone was screaming: 'Brad! Brad! Over here!' The flashbulbs are exploding in your face. Your adrenaline shoots sky-high, because people are just screaming." Brad's and Juliette's lives became a whirlwind of work, adventure and fun. The couple plunged into a roller-coaster romance that lasted three years.

For the first time in his young life, Brad felt content. He was dating a great girl and was finally happy with the way his career was going.

The excitement over *Thelma & Louise* didn't subside quickly. At Oscar time the movie was nominated for several awards, including Best Actress for both Geena Davis and Susan Sarandon. Coproducer and writer Callie Khouri won the Academy Award for Best Original Screenplay. The movie was listed as number 61 in *Entertainment Weekly*'s "100 Most Popular Films of All Time." *Thelma & Louise* was both a critical and a commercial hit. Though women liked the movie immediately, male viewers at first didn't appreciate this female version of *Butch Cassidy and the Sundance Kid*. By the time the video was released, however, everyone wanted to see it, and it eventually became a blockbuster hit.

Brad treasures *Thelma & Louise* as an experience that helped him grow as an actor and perfect his craft. "I enjoyed the whole experience. After the stuff I had done, it was a relief to be in something that important." He was onscreen for just fifteen minutes, but they became the most memorable minutes in the movie.

Thanks to the success of *Thelma & Louise,* Brad found himself the target of enormous attention over the next year. His role in the movie turned him from a small-time actor to a major player in the star game. But Brad wasn't ready to play in that game just yet.

seven

Pitt Stops

Immediately after he wrapped up the filming of his part in *Thelma & Louise,* Brad was eager to get started on another film. He tried out for the lead roles in two less-than-glamorous movies and won both parts. The first was the independent feature *Johnny Suede,* in which Brad played a teenager with an outrageously high pompadour who aspires to be a rock-and-roll singer like his idol, Ricky Nelson.

Cinematographer turned writer-director Tom DiCillo cast Brad but had a hard time convincing the backers of the film that "unknown Brad Pitt" was the right guy for the part. Later, after Brad's name had become a household word, DiCillo considered himself a very lucky first-time director to have nabbed such a star.

The movie, which reportedly had a budget of

only $500,000, had a lot going for it, most notably its star. On a visual level, it was an intriguing fable. It had a stylish, dreamlike mood and abstract dialogue. DiCillo played up Brad's comic timing; there were several funny moments. *Gilligan's Island* star Tina Louise appeared in a cameo. The film won the Golden Leopard for best picture at the Locarno, a key European festival whose competition is restricted to first and second films by new directors.

The buzz about *Johnny Suede* was so strong that the studio funded two big bicoastal premieres. At the L.A. premiere Brad, who attended with Juliette Lewis, said, "I'm happy with this movie. It's a fun one."

Looking very different from his onscreen character, Brad arrived wearing long hair parted in the middle and a beard and mustache. "I'm most comfortable in my boxers and wearing my hair natural," he told reporters, adding that his cinematic hair experience had been "close to torture. Someone was pulling on my head for two hours every day."

If that experience was hair-raising for Brad, it was nothing compared to working on his next movie, *Cool World*. The film, which combined live action with animation, was the brainchild of Ralph Bakshi, an animation director who brought

Lord of the Rings, *American Pop* and *Wizards* to the big screen. In *Cool World,* Gabriel Byrne played Jack Deebs, an underground cartoonist whose life unhinges when he finds himself in the cartoon world he created. Kim Basinger was Holli Would, a voluptuous cartoon character who wants to be human.

Brad played Detective Frank Harris, a tortured young victim of tragedy who seeks solace in the bizarre animated universe. He retreats into Cool World as a haven from feelings he doesn't want to experience. "My character took some hard knocks in his life, so he checked out," explained Brad. "And now he's in Cool World and it's really grand there. It's fantasy time."

Brad tried out for the movie because he was a fan of Ralph Bakshi and thought it would be a change of pace. In fact, everyone wanted to get involved with this project when it was first announced. "Everybody came into this movie because they just loved it," said producer Frank Mancuso, Jr. "Gabriel Byrne wanted to do it. After Kim Basinger read the script designed for her, she said, 'I'm in, boys.' "

Ralph Bakshi laughed later when he thought back on the early casting negotiations he had to go through for Brad. "I had seen about two hundred actors for the part. Like, *everyone*. Brad was a kid when I met him. He's going through the roof now, but he wasn't when we hired him. He was just a kid when he came in, you know, with his baseball hat on backwards. Brad walked in the room, did a reading and blew me away. I thought he was the only one who could do this part. He was a cross between a young Alan Ladd and James Dean. Brad could walk across a floor and be sensual without trying.''

Still, with all the praise Bakshi lavished on Brad, he had a tough time talking the money people into hiring the young actor. "The executives at the studio didn't see it at first," Bakshi continued. "We hired him and Brad turned out to be a really talented, great person in the role. A perfect fit.''

Brad was fascinated by the incredible amount of work it took to mix the live action with the animation. Most of his scenes were filmed in front of a blue screen, and that provided a new challenge for Brad, who had to play out scenes with invisible ''costars'' that would be drawn and added in later.

"If you have an ego, you'll lose it doing these kind of scenes," said Brad. "Where you have to put your arm around an invisible girl and kiss the air. With all these people on the set, you'll get humbled quick.'' Having to play love scenes and fight scenes with animated characters became an art in itself for Brad, who admitted, "It just became a dance."

Unfortunately, *Cool World*, which could have been a hip answer to *Who Framed Roger Rabbit*, never lived up to expectations. One industry insider said, "Nobody got out of that film alive, but Brad looked better than anyone else."

With *Johnny Suede* and *Cool World* Brad had taken a couple of chances and faced some disappointments. He was at a crucial point in his career. He had to be careful about the type of movie he would get involved with next. Luckily, just as he was deciding on his next career move, he got a call telling him that he had been cast in a new movie to be directed by Robert Redford. This proved to be his smartest move yet.

eight

A River Runs Through It

"I felt a bit of pressure on *A River Runs Through It*," Brad said. "And I thought that it was one of my weakest performances. It's so weird that it ended up being the one that I got the most attention for."

A River Runs Through It was the first movie of high quality that Brad carried almost entirely by himself, a fact that could rattle any young actor. The truth is that Brad did a magnificent job portraying charismatic but tragic Paul Maclean. The movie is an adaptation of Norman Maclean's autobiographical novella, which tells his younger brother's life story as well as depicting the difficulty everyone in the Maclean family had in expressing their feelings. The story takes place in Montana in the early 1900s. The only common ground between the brothers and their minister father seems to be the sport of fly-fishing.

It was crucial to find the right actors to play the three lead parts. Robert Redford, the film's director, easily settled on Tom Skerritt as Reverend Maclean and cast Craig Sheffer as Norman. But he was having trouble finding the right actor to play Paul. In his search, Redford wrote up a list of actors whose work he admired and who he thought were capable of playing demanding roles. Names like Kiefer Sutherland, Peter Gallagher, Robert Downey, Jr., and John Cusack appeared on the list.

Redford wasn't looking for a "star"; he was looking for an actor. He saw something in Brad the first day he met him. After just one meeting, Redford cast Brad as Paul.

Industry insiders have hinted that Redford cast Brad because Brad was on a hot streak after his performance in *Thelma & Louise*. But that was simply not the case. Redford's decision was based entirely on his meeting with Brad.

Coming face to face with Robert Redford made Brad a little nervous. After all, he would be talking to the man who directed *Ordinary People*, one of his favorite movies. But once the two golden-haired actors shook hands, Brad was completely at ease. In many ways, Brad reminded Redford of a younger version of himself.

"Once we cut through his nerves and insecurity, I felt there was something there that was very right for this part," Redford said of Brad. "I didn't want to see trouble on the face. Paul is a character with great light and energy. There was a lot of work that had to be done to bring that out in Brad because these young actors live in such different times. Today it's cool to brood and throw your lines away and act like you don't care. I just sensed that Brad wanted to be a truthful fellow. He was in a city with a lot of attitude, and he had to cut through that stuff."

Brad has always been able to slip easily into his characters, to become them and understand them, and he adapted quickly to his role in *A River Runs Through It*. He was drawn to the character from the start. It was probably an asset that, like Paul Maclean, Brad had been born and raised in a small town.

Describing his character, Brad said, "Paul's a guy who's got desires and beliefs that do not fall in with his family's plans or with the way he was raised. Paul has a loving but troubled relationship with his family. Because of that dilemma, he can never let it out completely, so there's always guilt and there's always pretense. If you're not allowed to be yourself, if you have to fake it to people

In 1993 Brad and Juliette Lewis journeyed to Las Vegas, where they were named Male and Female Star of Tomorrow by Nato ShoWest. (Copyright © 1993 by Connie Ives/Hot Shot Photos)

Brad is great with kids. When the little boy who played his son in *Legends of the Fall* was afraid to ride a horse in one scene, Brad was the one who was able to talk him into doing it. (Copyright © 1994 by Chris Helcermanas-Benge/Shooting Star)

Brad and his *Dallas* co-star Shalane McCall dated while they were on the show. Here the cute couple attend a March of Dimes Ski Event. (Copyright © 1988 by Bob Ives/Hot Shot Photos)

The cast of *Kalifornia* (left to right): Brad, Juliette Lewis, Michelle Forbes and David Duchovny. Brad and his then girlfriend Juliette broke up right after they finished filming this movie. (Copyright © 1993 by Polygram/Shooting Star)

Ever the perfectionist, Brad worked hard learning the art of fly-fishing for *A River Runs Through It*. His convincing performance as Paul Maclean turned him into the most sought-after actor in Hollywood. (Copyright © 1992 by Columbia Pictures/ Shooting Star)

The handsome Maclean brothers of *A River Runs Through It*: Craig Sheffer as Norman and Brad as Paul. (Copyright © 1992 by Columbia Pictures/Shooting Star)

Has success spoiled this sexy superstar? "No," said Brad. "My life is good. It hasn't changed much." (Copyright © 1994 by Bob Ives/Hot Shot Photos)

Brad Pitt: the hottest actor to hit the screen in years. (Copyright © 1995 by Erik Heinila/Shooting Star)

His fifteen-minute performance in *Thelma & Louise* had all of Hollywood asking, "Who is this guy?" For this scene with Geena Davis, Brad's main concern was that his mother wouldn't approve. (Copyright © 1991 by MGM/Shooting Star)

Brad, who played Louis in *Interview With the Vampire,* said of the film, "When I read the book, I thought it was great, and I think the movie is great. I'm really proud of it." (Copyright © 1994 by Geffen Pictures/Shooting Star)

"I've always thought there would be someone better for most of the roles I've taken. But I knew I was the best one to play Tristan," said Brad of his role in *Legends of the Fall*. (Copyright © 1994 by Chris Helcermanas-Benge /Shooting Star)

"I was so impressed with Christian Slater. He walked in like a pro, no ego or anything," said Brad, shown talking to his costar at the premiere of *Interview With the Vampire*. Christian stepped into the role that was to have been played by the late River Phoenix. (Copyright © 1994 by Connie Ives/Hot Shot Photos)

Brad has fond memories of his years at Kickapoo High School in Springfield, Missouri. The handsome honor student participated in many school activities, including student council, choir, speech and debate. Athletic Brad was also on the basketball, tennis and wrestling teams. (Copyright © 1995 by Seth Poppel/ Yearbook Archives)

Portrait of a young, aspiring actor: Clean-cut Brad looked like this when he began his acting career. (Copyright © 1988 by Connie Ives/Hot Shot Photos)

Brad has been linked with a string of beautiful women. He escorted ex-girlfriend Jitka Pohlodek to the premiere of *Legends of the Fall*. (Copyright © 1994 by Bob Ives/Hot Shot Photos)

Brad showed off a buzz-cut hair-style at the 1995 Golden Globe Awards. (Copyright © 1995 by Lisa O'Connor/Ace/Shooting Star)

who are very important to you, I think it leads to self-destruction sooner or later.''

In preparation for his role, Brad worked longest on learning the art of fly-fishing, since it was an important part of his character. A few weeks before leaving for Montana, Brad practiced his casting with a fly rod on top of Hollywood buildings. ''I'd hook myself in the back of my head all the time,'' he admitted. ''One time, they had to dig the barb out with pliers.''

When *A River Runs Through It* was unleashed on moviegoers, it received terrific reviews and did good business at the box office. Word of mouth may in the end have been the reason for its success. The photography was breathtaking, especially when viewed on a big screen. More like a European movie than anything Hollywood was turning out, this beautiful piece of filmmaking grossed a tidy $43 million.

The real bait was Brad, who was now being compared to the young Redford. His performance was hailed by critics, but surprisingly, the star himself wasn't satisfied. ''There could have been more underneath. A little more back-story,'' Brad said, describing his part in the film. ''But there was no getting around it. Redford did a fantastic job crafting that film, shaping it into chiseled granite. A film adapted from a book has to take its own form. Redford did that.''

On the set of *River,* Brad got along with all the stars but became buddies with an actor who had just one line. Buck Simmons was on a break from college and was traveling through Montana when he saw an ad for a fly fisherman who could act. Buck auditioned and won a speaking role in the movie.

After becoming friends with Brad, Buck got the bug to give acting a more serious try. He moved to Hollywood and then into Brad's three-bedroom house in West Hollywood, where he shared the rent. Unfortunately, not all actors who chase after their dream in Hollywood get work, and Buck fell into this category.

Brad hoped the movie's success would start the ball rolling for Hollywood to produce other projects of similar quality. "No one expected *River* to do well at the box office," he said. "Redford's proved that you can elevate film with really good material."

The fact that Brad didn't pause to savor his success before plunging into his next movie was not a surprise. Ambitious and determined, Brad once again did the opposite of what was expected. In a daring move, he accepted the role of a psycho killer in *Kalifornia.* Would this decision jeopardize his new golden-boy image? He would soon find out!

nine

A Different Direction

There were two reasons why Brad wanted to play homicidal drifter Early Grayce in the small, offbeat movie *Kalifornia*. One was to show his versatility as an actor; the other was to work on a new project with his girlfriend Juliette Lewis.

Brad and Juliette had been dating almost three years and were the hottest couple in Hollywood. They regularly showed up at public events together and developed a reputation as a cozy twosome who seemed to be genuinely in love. The bond between Brad and Juliette was obvious. Despite the ten-year difference in their ages, they shared many interests.

In the fall of 1992 they moved into a house in the Hollywood Hills and attempted to furnish it with all the things they loved. Brad brought his three dogs, and Juliette brought her cat, Me. The couple enjoyed shopping in antiques stores on weekends and buying old furniture like red upholstered chairs and Tiffany lamps. They each had a large collection of books, which they arranged in floor-to-ceiling bookshelves in a room designed just for reading. They piled up their scripts on a low wood chest Brad bought.

Though they worked in the same business, Brad said, there was no competition between them. Brad was in awe of Juliette's acting talents, and she felt the same way about him. They were interested in the same kinds of projects.

Brad and Juliette often talked about working together again. With his performance in *A River Runs Through It* and her Oscar-nominated one in *Cape Fear,* they became two of the most respected and talented young stars in the business. Nato ShoWest in Las Vegas named them Male and Female Star of Tomorrow. The accolades were coming their way fast and furious. But they yearned for more.

Juliette was ready to play a real character part; Brad just wanted to take his career in a different direction. When *Kalifornia* came along, they knew they had found what they were looking for, and they expressed immediate interest.

By this time, Brad was established as one of Hollywood's brightest young stars, and he knew the time was right to show what else he was capable of doing. After working with Robert Redford and Ridley Scott, Brad was advised against working on *Kalifornia* with first-time director Dominic Sena.

One of the rules of the game is to get big-name directors interested and then to *keep* them interested. It's rare for an actor to start at the top and work his way *down* from big-budget movies to low-budget independents. Once a young actor's career is on a roll, he doesn't look back. But that has never been Brad's style. His philosophy is: If the film is good, he's interested. If a character presents him with a new challenge, it doesn't really matter how big or small the role is.

Brad wanted to do the movie *Kalifornia*, and he wasn't about to let anyone talk him out of it. "You want to show what you can do," he said. "You want to do something different from the last one, before they think they know what you're about. This role was the farthest thing from golden boy."

The sensitivity Brad displayed in *A River Runs Through It* disappeared in *Kalifornia*. And that was just what Brad hoped for. "I wanted to do one of those trailer-dwelling, greasy-nails guys— no education, canned food, real white trash," he said, then added, "You almost *have* to see *Kalifornia*."

Kalifornia is the story of Brian Kessler (David Duchovny) and Carrie Laughlin (Michelle Forbes), a fledgling writer and photographer. When Brian lands a contract to write a book based on a magazine article he wrote about murder, he decides he and Carrie should work on it together. Using his words and her photos, they set out to explore famous murder sites on their way to a new life in California. Trying to save money, they advertise for another couple to travel with them.

Early Grayce (Brad) and his naive girlfriend, Adele Corners (Juliette), answer the ad. Unknown to Brian and Carrie, Early is about to take them all on what could be their last journey. Though Carrie is uneasy about the couple's coming along, they seem normal enough in the beginning. No one realizes until it's too late that Early is dangerous and they have become unwilling accomplices in a cross-country murder spree. By the movie's end, all their lives are in jeopardy as they become Early's prisoners.

Although *Kalifornia* is about the lives of the four characters, Brad's performance is so strong he nearly overshadows the other three actors.

The movie, which was lauded at the Montreal Film Festival, is clearly one of Brad's favorites.

"It's a four-character piece, a quartet," he said. "It's really interesting that the other couple are very hip, very New York. In a sense, they've had every advantage. Then you have this white-trash couple hanging out. A lot of it is really sweet, believe it or not."

Brad continued, "Could I have played the good guy in *Kalifornia*? Sure. But I needed to play the bad guy. I needed the balance. I don't believe in the all-your-eggs-in-one-bucket kind of theory. You get pushed in this business, you just have to push back harder. Because it comes down to you. People have different takes on things, people have good takes. But only you know about your own deal—your own creativity."

Brad immersed himself in the role. He gained twenty pounds, let his hair get long and grew a goatee. Still, women on the set swooned over him. Dominic Sena said of Brad, "This guy just gets through to women, no matter what."

Brad's portrayal of the menacing outlaw Early has been called his best performance to date, and it was one of the first that seemed to please him. Even though his character is a cold-blooded criminal, Brad was quick to defend him. "There's no such thing as not having a conscience," he said. "Somehow you block it off. Every human has a soul. It's easy to look at someone disgusting and think whatever, but when you get underneath the surface, why they move this way or why they breathe, you fall for them."

As for the filming, Brad said at the time, "It's been a fun shoot, because it's been so easy and I get to hang out with my love." A short time later, in February 1993, Brad and Juliette broke up. Their separation came as a complete surprise to everyone around them.

What caused the split between Brad and Juliette as they reached the end of filming *Kalifornia*? Friends of the couple said they were talking marriage one day and the next were going their separate ways. Not long before they broke up, Juliette had been telling friends and reporters that she and Brad were going to get married, claiming he brought out a softer, more domestic side of her. "We've talked and we both know we're each other's person for life," she said. "I love to bake him pies and make him tea at night. I wasn't domestic until I fell in love. We're fifty million times stronger and more in love than when we started."

One of Juliette's friends said she was "extraordinarily intense" about her relationship with Brad and was upset when it came to an end.

It's ironic that they met while working on their TV movie and broke up, three years later, after working together again. "I still love the woman," Brad said recently. "There's some real genius there. I had a great time with her. I don't want to go into an explanation. She has her own views, and I respected those views. It was one of the greatest relationships I've ever been in. The problem is, we grow up with this vision that love conquers all, and that's just not so."

Maybe it was the breakup with Juliette that led Brad to slow down for one year and work only when he wanted to. He was searching for a great role, but it took him more than a year to find it. In the meantime, he accepted a part in the giddy love romp *The Favor*. It's the only movie he has done that centers on love and marriage.

At the audition, writer Joseann McGibbon remembered, Brad wore a hat and a T-shirt with Disney's seven dwarfs imprinted on it. Harley Jane Kozak, one of the movie's stars, gushed, "He was adorable. I desperately wanted to be ten years younger."

The movie was directed by Donald Petrie, who cast Julia Roberts in one of her first roles in his 1988 movie *Mystic Pizza*. Petrie immediately noticed Brad's appeal and star quality. Naturally, Brad did a perfect reading for the role of the twenty-six-year-old artist Elliott and was cast. "It was the unpredictability of his interpretation," said Petrie. "Nine out of ten actors read for a role the way you'd expect. But Brad was a little off, a little quirky."

Taking the role of Elliott in *The Favor* was not one of Brad's better decisions, although he enjoyed working on the film. When it was released, it received less than glowing reviews; most critics were surprised to see Brad in such a thankless role.

He followed up *The Favor* with a tiny part in *True Romance,* which starred Christian Slater and was written by Quentin Tarantino of *Pulp Fiction* fame. Brad played Floyd, a grungy, laid-back denizen of the Hollywood Hills who spends the majority of his time onscreen lounging on a sofa. Brad took the small part because, like others in the film, he wanted to play one of Quentin Tarantino's unusual characters.

The supporting cast of *True Romance* are all accomplished actors, mostly stars. Gary Oldman, Dennis Hopper and Val Kilmer have small roles. There was constant excitement on the set, and Brad said of the experience, "That was fun. But I was only there for a couple of days."

Taking these minor roles said something about Brad Pitt. He could have been writing his own ticket and going out for major movies, but he chose instead to play offbeat characters. Having made up his mind to do his own thing, he hoped it would lead to a long career as an actor.

He was hungry to do another movie that would give him the acting challenges he had enjoyed in the past, but he was in no hurry. "After a while, you get the feeling that you have to start choosing the best of what's available," he said. "The typical hero with the cool one-liners just doesn't interest me. I'd rather see people dealing with problems, trying to get around them. There's places for both kinds of roles, but what I respect is this thing of seeing people trying."

It was a lucky thing Brad took it slow for a year. When the year had passed, he plunged into not one but two physically and emotionally demanding roles in two powerful movies.

ten

Legends of the Fall

The year 1993 was a busy and momentous one for Brad. He was not only the first actor cast in the eagerly awaited *Interview With the Vampire*, but he also won the coveted part of Tristan in the romantic epic *Legends of the Fall*.

The latter movie was more important to him because he had worked more than a year campaigning for the role. He said he knew the character of Tristan inside and out from the moment he first read the script. "Films are exhausting to make," he said, "so you'd better pick something that means something to you, and this one did. It is a very true account of living and dying and the journey along the way. It made sense to me.

"This story was one of the only ones where I've ever said, 'I'm the guy for this one.' I've always thought there would be someone better for most of the roles I've taken. But I knew I was the best one to play Tristan. I knew the corners, the bends in the road, knew exactly where it went. My difficulty was trying to get others to see it the way I did."

When casting for *Legends of the Fall* began, Brad's name came up as a candidate for the role of Tristan. Director Edward Zwick and producer Marshall Herskovitz, the *Legends* team who created the TV series *Thirtysomething* and *My So-Called Life*, both remembered Brad from his one-line guest spot on *Thirtysomething* in 1989. "He caused such a stir on the set," said Herskovitz. "He was so good-looking and so charismatic and such a sweet guy, everybody knew he was going places."

They were anxious to meet Brad again, and when they did they knew he was the right actor to play Tristan. "Brad had a very strong, intuitive understanding of this character," said Zwick. "I think there is a great deal of Tristan within him. I know he has challenged himself to explore some of the darker aspects of his character as well as the more romantic qualities."

On this movie Brad was not just an actor. To bring the epic to the screen, Brad and Edward Zwick had to strike a lucrative deal. The director said, "One way we got this movie made was for

Brad and me to defer a significant part of our salaries, and for Brad to become my partner.''

This gave Brad some say in production, but not as much as he would have liked. For one, he lobbied to get Aidan Quinn the role of Alfred, which Brad called "the toughest part in the movie. It could have easily gone wimpy. And we needed somebody who'd be equal to Tristan, bring nobility and strength to the role, and sexiness, of all things, and that's Aidan. Somebody give this guy an Oscar. I mean, it's time."

Aidan was blown away when he learned that Brad thought so highly of his work. "He actually called the studio to get me hired," said Aidan. "They wanted a bigger name, but he wanted me. We both have brothers, so that sort of connected us to the story. We had extraordinary support for each other and lots of laughs."

Based on Jim Harrison's 1979 novella of the same title and set in Montana in the early 1900s, *Legends of the Fall* is the story of three brothers who all love the same woman. Colonel William Ludlow (Anthony Hopkins) is a U.S. Cavalry officer who is fed up with the government's treatment of Native Americans. He retires and sets out to raise his three sons on a ranch in the remote foothills of the Montana Rockies.

The brothers are Alfred (Aidan Quinn), the

oldest and most reserved; the much-loved Samuel (Henry Thomas); and Tristan (Brad), the tormented middle brother who is unlike the others. He is a wild, untamable youth who learns the skills and the nature of a warrior from his father's Cree scout, One Stab (Gordon Tootoosis). The three brothers are inseparable until they are torn apart by World War I. At the center of the brothers' sudden rivalry is Susannah (Julia Ormond), the woman they all love.

When the film was first announced, the role of Susannah became the most sought-after part in Hollywood. More than a dozen young actresses were up for the role, including Nicole Kidman, but twenty-nine-year-old British newcomer Julia Ormond won it.

The only problem was that TriStar wasn't completely comfortable with the casting of an unknown to play the love of Brad's life. Edward Zwick quickly shot a screen test of Julia, and the studio executives were convinced. "Julia," said Brad, "has this kind of timeless class I haven't seen anywhere else."

Julia was equally impressed with Brad. "I think Brad has something very special," she said. "Apart from the fact that he is a gorgeous guy, he's also someone who's constantly trying to shrug it off. He's not egotistical. He's very, very careful with people—and sweet.''

Because of their obvious chemistry onscreen, there were rumors that Brad and Julia were carrying their passion into their offscreen lives. The rumor got its start in a logical place: Brad shared a rented house with Julia during the filming. Brad didn't realize this arrangement would be leaked to the press. After all, everyone involved claimed the relationship was platonic. Director Edward Zwick insisted, "They were only roommates, not lovers."

Still, the two actors' living arrangement was reported immediately by the local media. A journalist followed Brad home one night after a long day of filming. Brad was completely exhausted and in no mood to answer the questions of a reporter looking for a juicy scoop. He calmly said to the writer, "Don't do this. I'll give you an interview later."

On the set, Brad saw to it that other actors felt comfortable. Karina Lombard, who played Tristan's wife, learned a lot from Brad. Her role was an extremely challenging one, and Karina needed complete concentration. She has credited Brad with teaching her the fundamental secret of ignoring the usual chaos on the set and focusing on her character.

"I learned something from Brad," she said. "To just be in the moment, to not care about the yapping that is always going on around the set. To just be yourself, and not care who says what and who wants what. It's a great gift to be able to do your stuff and not give a damn what others think."

For the most part, it was pretty easy going for Brad. He got to ride horses, and he did most of his own stunts. He was thrilled to be working with Oscar winner Anthony Hopkins *(The Silence of the Lambs)*. Hopkins took the role in *Legends* because he was a big fan of Western movies and had always dreamed of being in one. "There's something very romantic about the West and these great spectacles," he says.

One of Edward Zwick's main concerns was keeping the production on schedule. Most of the scenes were shot near Calgary, Alberta, Canada. It rained nonstop for most of the first two months. The cast and crew tried to ignore the gallons of rain that fell by adjusting their schedules and working overtime once the sun came out.

Brad held Saturday-night jam sessions at his rented house, at which all the actors got out of their Western garb and enjoyed the music and singing. Everything seemed to be running smoothly for Brad. And then he ran into an obstacle.

It had been reported that Brad and his director didn't always see eye to eye during filming. But tensions really began flaring during a few crucial scenes. Because of the torrential rain, all the scenes were shot out of order. Though most movies are filmed out of sequence, it was especially difficult to film *Legends* this way because the script was being rewritten during the filming.

One of the problems was "Scene 202: Jail Cell—Susannah visits Tristan in jail." The scene comes near the end of the movie. Tristan is in jail, and Susannah, married to Alfred, is tormented by her love for Tristan. Because of the rain, the scene had to be shot during the first week of filming. "At that point, the jail scene wasn't right, wasn't written right, didn't fit in," said Brad. "When we shot it, I said, 'This is a mistake.' But Edward Zwick wanted to shoot it."

What followed was a disagreement between Brad and his director that was so explosive the crew scuttled away. According to one crew member, a chair was tossed, but it certainly wasn't thrown *at* anybody.

Zwick has admitted the argument happened. "Sure, we went at it, and that is part of the process," he said. "Certainly by the next morning we were contrite and desperately eager to make up, not hold on to it, and go on to the next big thing.''

Brad, who believes disagreements on the set are fine and actually help a production, commented, ''Ed and I had a tough day that day, which is good. It's good if two people care. Have at it because at the end you're going to come up with something good—and that was the result in the jail scene we ended up with. It was written right and it was done right.''

Another major disagreement between Brad and Zwick occurred when Brad found out that a good chunk of his best acting was not going to make it into the final cut of the film. Most of the scenes of Tristan's sinking into madness and slowly recovering from it were cut.

Brad wasn't at all pleased with the director's decision to slice up his scenes in favor of developing other characters. ''By taking out so much, as they did, the movie becomes too mushy, because there's no space in between the mush,'' he said. ''If I'd known where it was going to end up, I would have really fought against the cheese. The Kraft Macaroni Deluxe Dinner. The movie's not cheesy by any means. This is a good movie. There are just moments where, if it was reduced to that, if that's all we were going to see of him, I would have whittled it down. I wouldn't have shown so much."

Regardless of their disagreements on the set, Brad and Edward Zwick parted pals. Zwick praised his star's performance as outstanding. Though all the performances in *Legends* are strong, Zwick considered the movie a star-making vehicle for Brad.

"It's undeniable," said Zwick. "His physicality—the riding and stunts—juxtaposed with his vulnerability succeeds in painting a picture of a man who is a force of nature."

Aidan Quinn believes Brad came of age in this film, especially in a scene where he's in a graveyard. "I happened onto some dailies that were on tape, and saw him at that grave and he was just devastating," said Aidan. "Brad's got a very traditional manly kind of persona, so to see him fighting the emotion and not winning—there was stuff he was adding that wasn't scripted—was just so powerful, watching it spill out."

Brad has called *Legends of the Fall* an "epic saga. You know that's the deal where you start out with one grave and by the end there's twenty-three." He likes to talk about *Legends of the Fall;* he is extremely proud of it. "A lot of the elements are very strange—Western, war, love triangle, family, killings," he says. "It's bold, it's big, like a great bottle of wine."

Brad desperately wanted to see the results of his work on *Legends,* but the movie was not released until more than a year after the production wrapped. Brad had gotten Tristan out of his system by the end of summer 1993; audiences would not see the movie until December 1994. By the time it was released, *Legends of the Fall* was an eagerly awaited star vehicle, and Brad Pitt's name was a household word.

eleven

Interview With the Vampire

As the *Legends of the Fall* shoot neared its end, Brad was drained. His one wish was to take a much-needed vacation, but he knew a trip would have to wait because he was committed to playing Louis in *Interview With the Vampire*.

After finishing *Legends* in Calgary, Brad got on a plane to New Orleans, where production was to begin on *Interview With the Vampire*. This back-to-back filming schedule proved extremely grueling. He thought he was ready to sink his teeth into the role of the suicidal vampire Louis. In reality, it was the most difficult part he had ever played.

Director Neil Jordan (*The Crying Game*) said, "Brad really suffered the role. He came into it totally exhausted from doing *Legends*. He did agonize."

Brad just had time to read through the script on the plane and clean what he called "the hick" out of his voice. As he started to play Louis, the character really began to depress him. It didn't make it any easier that he appears in almost every scene.

"I hated doing this movie. Hated it," Brad asserted. "I loved watching it. Completely. But I hated doing it. My character is depressed from the beginning to the end. Five and a half months of that was just too much."

He went on to talk in detail about Louis and the reason why the role bothered him so much. "My character wants to kill himself for the whole movie. I've never thought about killing myself. It was a sick thing. I don't like when a movie messes with your day."

A dark cloud seemed to hang over Brad for the entire filming of *Interview*. He was very insecure and questioned his acting abilities constantly. Neil Jordan said, "He was totally immersed in the role. A vampire never sees the light, and that's how Brad was in this shoot."

Interview With the Vampire begins in the eighteenth century and centers on Louis De Ponte Du Lac (Brad), a New Orleans plantation owner who seeks a release from his suffering after the death of his wife and infant daughter. A chance encounter brings him into contact with Lestat, who offers him a life beyond what he has known—as a vampire. Once bitten by Lestat, Louis becomes increasingly guilty about his new existence. To relieve him of his loneliness, Lestat transforms one of his victims, five-year-old Claudia (Kirsten Dunst), into a third vampire so that she can become Louis's permanent companion. Two hundred years later, in twentieth-century San Francisco, Louis decides to tell his story to a young reporter, Malloy (Christian Slater). It is a story of desire, love, grief, terror and ecstasy.

Brad Pitt was the name on everyone's list for the role of Louis. Neil Jordan said, "I've seen everything Brad has done, and he is just absolutely captivating." Producer Stephen Woolley said, "Brad had been discussed from day one as someone we all thought would be good as Louis. There is a certain vulnerability to the character which is very important, and Brad has that side to his nature."

With Brad set to play Louis, the moviemakers still hadn't found an actor to portray Lestat. Daniel Day-Lewis kept them waiting for six months until he finally withdrew from the project. The filmmakers thought of Mel Gibson, William Baldwin and Ralph Fiennes, star of *Quiz Show* and a costar in *Schindler's List*. Then the idea of

Tom Cruise came up in a conversation. Casting director Juliet Taylor said, "Neil, Stephen and I told David Geffen about Tom and he really loved it." Geffen decided to give Tom Cruise a call. He had worked with Cruise before in the actor's early breakthrough movie, *Risky Business,* and he remembered him as a consummate professional.

For the role of Claudia, the filmmakers decided to cast Kirsten Dunst, a young actress from Point Pleasant, New Jersey, who had only minor credits to her name. More than five hundred children auditioned; Kirsten was the first actress they thought enough of to videotape.

Kirsten had been spotted by talent scouts while shopping in Beverly Hills with her mother. "They asked me if I was an actor," said Kirsten. "They told us that I should try out for *Interview With the Vampire.*" The idea excited her. "I always wanted to be a vampire," she said. "Before this movie, I dreamed about it. I pictured me with fangs."

On the day she was to film her screen test, Tom Cruise arrived to watch. Seeing Tom and Kirsten in the same room clinched the decision. "Kirsten and Tom looked so good together," said Joanna Colbert, a former associate of casting director Taylor. "You just didn't know who was in what role. Is she the one seducing him or is he seducing her?''

While many girls have pictures of Tom Cruise and Brad Pitt on their bedroom walls, Kirsten seemed unfazed at finding herself working with two of Hollywood's hottest hunks. "I like Brad and Tom because they're nice, and they're generous and care about me," she said. "Not because they're hot.''

While her friends back home would have given their eyeteeth to kiss Brad onscreen, Kirsten claimed she didn't particularly enjoy it. "The real reason is that I consider Brad to be like my big brother,'' she said.

Kirsten established quite a rapport with Brad and Tom. In their offscreen time, the three stars took Polaroid pictures of each other making funny faces and stuck them on a board they called the ugly wall. "Brad acted more like a twelve-year-old than a thirty-one-year-old,'' said Kirsten, laughing.

With all the principal characters cast, production on *Interview* began on October 18, 1993, in New Orleans. Filming lasted more than five months and took place in four locations: New Orleans, San Francisco, Paris and England's Pinewood Studios. Forty days of night shooting were required to get the dark, eerie feeling the filmmakers wanted. Brad spent the first couple of days shooting close-ups that had to be reshot because his vampire makeup turned out to be too heavy.

Though the cameras rolled, the movie was not free of trouble. Only two weeks after filming started, the shocking news came that River Phoenix, who had been cast as the young reporter, had died. The news hit Brad especially hard because he had thought River was one of the few promising young actors in Hollywood. He had looked forward to meeting River and working with him on *Interview*.

"I knew River a little, but I wanted to know him more," said Brad. "His death affected everyone on the movie, but at the same time it was real personal. You have to realize, River did a role in *My Own Private Idaho* that took it to a level that none of these other young guys have gotten to yet. I was really looking forward to him being on the set. It just seems like when we lost him, we all lost something special."

The untimely death of River Phoenix sent the filmmakers into a frenzy. His role, though small, was vital to the movie, and they needed to find a young actor fast. Rising star Leonardo DiCaprio and Stephen Dorff both read for the role. DiCaprio really wanted it, and although he was brilliant, he was far too young. David Geffen decided on Christian Slater, who was apprehensive about stepping into River's part.

Brad had worked with Christian on the movie *True Romance,* but he didn't know him well. "It was a tough spot for him," said Brad about Christian's first day on the set. "It was the end of the film, everyone was just looking to get done, River's gone. He came in and was just a real person. He walked in like a pro, no ego or anything."

As the filming neared its end, rumors started to leak out from the set into the newspapers. The big one was that Brad and Tom Cruise weren't getting along. It's not clear how this story got started. Tom and Brad did spend some time together off camera. They raced go-carts in England—Cruise always won—and had a great time with Kirsten, whom they both adored. Director Neil Jordan admitted to being surprised when he first heard the stories, and he quickly came to the defense of his two young stars.

"Brad and Tom are two very different actors. And their characters were very different. Tom's character loves control and loves inflicting pain on Brad's character. Brad's character just wants to escape. In many ways they related to each other the way their characters did."

Brad, who said he thought Tom's performance was stirring, denied that there was tension between them. One report had to do with the fact that Tom is three inches shorter than Brad. Because Cruise thought he should be as tall as his costar, he reportedly had platform heels added to his boots. Costume designer Sandy Powell, who couldn't keep any of her production sketches, said, "You're not going to get me to talk about that."

But Brad doesn't mind giving his side of the story. "It's something people want to make a big deal of," he said. "He wanted his character to be more physically dominant. It does make sense . . . and then it doesn't."

Tom Cruise and Brad Pitt are as different as night and day. Though Brad is just one year younger than Tom, he was a struggling actor doing bit parts on TV when Tom was already breaking box-office records with movies like *Risky Business* and *Top Gun*. Tom is the 1980s-style hardworking, ambitious yuppie, always pushing himself to the limit, while Brad fits better into the 1990s style; he's laid-back and sweet. Their killer sex appeal is about the only thing these two actors have in common.

Brad described their differences this way: "He's the North Pole, I'm the South. He's coming at you with a handshake where I may bump into you, I may not, you know? I always thought there was this underlying competition that got in the way of any real conversation. It wasn't nasty by any means. But it was just *there* and it bugged me a bit. But I'll tell you, he catches a lot of heat because he's on top. He is a good actor and he advances in the film. You have to respect him for that."

What Brad couldn't get used to was the complete control Tom demanded during filming. He wanted a closed set and a promise that everyone involved with the production would remain silent about it. Cast and crew had to sign forms promising not to reveal the smallest bit of information. Tom had a covered canvas passageway set up from his trailer to the set so that no one could see him in makeup. Even Kirsten and Brad had to be brought to the set through the canvas tunnel. After a tabloid TV show managed to get a glimpse of Cruise as Lestat, security at Pinewood Studios really tightened up.

Neil Jordan, who by this time was tired of all the negative press, said, "Everyone who was a vampire was ferried onto the sets through the tunnel. We didn't want any photographs out of context and didn't want anyone copying us."

These were not the kind of surroundings Brad

had been used to. The atmosphere on the sets of his previous films had been fun. He might have disagreed with directors, but he had never worked under such tension. He didn't blame this all on Tom Cruise, but he did comment on Tom a few months later. "The machine Tom runs is quite impressive, but I wouldn't want to live like that," Brad said. "I like the guy, I honestly like the guy. But at a point I started really resenting him. In retrospect I realize that it was completely because of who our characters were. I realize that it was my problem. People take everything so seriously. It's a movie, and it's done."

When the movie finally premiered in November 1994 it was clear that it had elevated Brad to superstar status. *Interview With the Vampire* had a $36.4-million opening weekend and would eventually gross more than $100 million.

Only a couple of weeks later, still reeling from the success of *Interview,* Brad attended the premiere of *Legends of the Fall.* This was the movie that convinced the world Brad Pitt was here to stay!

twelve

Rebel or Golden Boy?

In the 1950s James Dean touched the lives of young people everywhere. He was called a rebel; he was an actor who seemed to speak to an entire generation. When he died in a car accident at the age of twenty-four, he might have faded from everyone's thoughts. But his impact had been too strong. The James Dean cult has endured for forty years, and his influence can still be felt in Hollywood. Since he died in 1955, every young actor with loads of talent and cool hair has been dubbed "the new James Dean."

Naturally, when Brad Pitt started attracting attention, this label was pinned on him. It was even hinted that J.D., his character in *Thelma & Louise*, borrowed his initials from the legendary star. Brad has been called "this generation's

James Dean," but he is not at all flattered by the comparison.

"It amazes me all these actors try to impersonate James Dean instead of finding out who they are," he said. "They ride around on their Harleys and they won't bathe. They're just trying to live this dream. Why would you want to pattern your life after someone who wasn't a survivor?"

Brad was a little more flattered to be compared to golden boy Robert Redford because he believes Redford has contributed greatly to movies as an actor, producer and director. Brad has never understood why James Dean went down in film history when he completed only three movies.

Since hitting it big, Brad has had many titles added to his name. He's been called golden boy, rebel, hunk and heartthrob. But he shrugs them all off. Brad just wants to be an actor. "I don't want people to think I'm the next big anything," he said. "Heartthrobs are a dime a dozen."

Nor is he that impressed with the young Hollywood stars of today. His favorite actors are the ones who inspired him while he was growing up; he doesn't see that much inspiration on the screen lately.

"Don't you ever wonder where the young Pacinos, the young De Niros, the young Newmans, the young Redfords are?" he asked. "Who do we have now that's young and inspiring? Sean Penn took a break. Don't get me wrong, there are a few, but not enough. We have Gary Oldman, and he's not that young, really. Juliette is one, and Dermot Mulroney.

"I want to see that collection of actors get strong," he continued. "I'd like to be inspired again. I don't see a lot of intelligence today."

Brad is too modest to include himself on this list of young Hollywood talent. He has an amazingly down-to-earth attitude about his gifts and the stardom he has achieved.

He may be living his dream, but it hasn't come without tension and sacrifice. By sticking to his philosophy of "not taking myself too seriously," Brad has said, he's been able to handle the mounting pressure. From his first rush of success, he has maintained a low profile. Since becoming a celebrity, he is even more intense about his time off and his privacy.

So what is the *real* Brad Pitt like when the cameras are turned off? First and foremost, his family is extremely important to him. They all still live in Missouri, and Brad makes a conscious effort to keep in close contact with them even when he's away on location. He surprised the entire Pitt clan by flying them out to Los Angeles for the premiere of *Legends of the Fall*. His brother, Doug, who owns a computer company, brought along his wife. Brad's sister, Julie, was only five weeks away from giving birth. The premiere was an exhilarating and momentous night for Brad, and he was happy to have his family share it with him.

Though he now lives in California, Brad will never stray too far from his family. He recently bought 600 acres of land near Springfield, Missouri, and plans to build a house on it which he dreams of using for family reunions.

Off camera, Brad Pitt is not a Hollywood guy who rides around town in huge limos. He's just a country boy who's enjoying all the good things that have come his way. Though he often seems very serious, he says nothing could be further from the truth.

"When I give interviews and give my life views, it sounds like I'm walking around like a prophet," he said. "And that's not true because most of the time I'm out cutting up, laughing and speeding in my car."

Brad drives a beat-up Jeep Cherokee. The outside is in need of a new paint job and the inside is littered with Brad's stuff, but he hasn't traded it in yet for a new set of wheels. He doesn't see the need to spend thousands on a new car to get him from one place to another. "I can't justify spending twenty grand on a truck," he said, but quickly added, "I would spend it on a Tiffany stained-glass window. I could completely justify that."

As when he lived with Juliette Lewis, Brad can often be spotted hunting down bargains at thrift shops or antiques stores. "The quality of things, if they're handmade, really impresses me," he said. "Just to have furniture made from first-growth trees, which we don't have anymore. The texture is different and the wood is different. It's a big difference from the little bitty grain we get here."

Lately Brad has been purchasing furniture for the house he recently moved into. It's an old mansion previously owned by Elvira, the TV horror hostess. As you might expect, the house and its surroundings were designed to suit Elvira's spooky persona, but Brad finds it all very intriguing.

Set behind a green iron gate with a spiderweb pattern, the three-story structure was built in 1910 and has well-crafted terraces and balconies all around it. Outside, there are a pool, a pond and a small man-made cave, which Brad enjoys so much that he decorated it with an oriental rug.

In the backyard Brad lets his menagerie of exotic pets run around. Thirty-five chameleons live in big wooden cages that look like Japanese lanterns. Brad owns iguanas, bobcats and three hound dogs named Todd Potter, Saudi and Purty. One of Brad's biggest concerns was "keeping the bobcats completely free. Not caged in like a bird, which blows my mind, cutting its wings."

Brad has begun furnishing his house with leather sofas and old wooden chairs and tables. One of the first things he set up in the house was his stereo. He owns a few hundred CDs, which he placed in no particular order on the shelves of a built-in glass cabinet. "It's kind of like you're on the search. You find the right CD for the moment," he said.

He is passionate about music; he plays CDs constantly. His taste in music runs to rock, jazz and blues. Among his favorites are Jimi Hendrix, Stone Temple Pilots, Gipsy Kings, Sade and Bob Marley. Brad owns three guitars and hasn't completely ruled out the idea of breaking into the music business. Even recently, when asked if he'd rather be a movie star or a rock star, he answered, "Are you kidding? A rock star. I want to do a male version of Marianne Faithfull's 'Why'd Ya Do It?'"

Up close, Brad is bigger than you might expect:

six feet tall and 155 pounds. He is even more handsome in person than he is on the big screen, especially when he flashes his trademark smile. You can get lost in his dreamy blue eyes.

Brad's love of architecture and drawing has never diminished. He sketches in his spare time and continues to study art. Strange things intrigue him—sharks, for example. He claimed he's really afraid of them but was glued to Shark Week on the Discovery Channel because "it was really fascinating."

Brad loves to dance and is very good at it. He said eating takes up too much of his time, and he's often satisfied with just a waffle for breakfast and a salami-on-bagel sandwich for lunch and even dinner. He sleeps in strange positions and often wakes up from vivid dreams.

Some of Brad's vices are chewing gum constantly, smoking and drinking lots of coffee and lots of soda—especially Mountain Dew and Coke. Brad packs his refrigerator with cold cuts, mustard, bottles of Evian water and soda. His kitchen shelves are lined with cans of dog food and furniture polish.

Believe it or not, the sexiest actor in Hollywood likes to stay home and polish the tables and chairs he buys. Most of the time you'll find him home rather than out on the town like other young stars. Now that he's finally getting himself settled into his own house (he had been renting bachelor pads all over West Hollywood), he likes to stay there. "I just reached a point where I have fun in a box by myself," he said.

With a schedule that is booked solid for the next two years, Brad is learning to adjust—and to relax. His emotions have been put on overdrive, and it's all been amazing for this usually easygoing guy. His own drive and sense of commitment catapulted him to his astounding success, but Brad sometimes has to give himself time to catch his breath. "I never knew I would achieve all of this," he admitted. "I never thought I'd get to the point where I was fulfilling all my dreams. It's been pretty overwhelming!"

thirteen

Hollywood Heartbreaker

He's the world's sexiest and most eligible bachelor. But Brad Pitt has not found the woman he wants to settle down with yet. He's dated a bevy of beautiful actresses, but this Hollywood heartthrob isn't seeing anyone steadily.

The folks back in his hometown say he was always a ladies' man, even as a teenager. "Brad broke a lot of young girls' hearts in Springfield, Missouri," said Brad's sister, Julie.

Perhaps because he grew up in a household with a mother and sister, Brad has always been very comfortable around members of the opposite sex. When he got out to Hollywood, this romantic, fun-loving guy dated many of the young women he worked with. But he was just having a good time. Now these past relationships have surfaced in the headlines and prompted the press to dub Brad "the number one heartbreaker in Hollywood."

A person in Brad's position creates a special mystique. The fact that he is considered the sexiest man in the world ignites stories that he is a ladykiller, that he has loved and then left a string of women all over Hollywood.

According to Brad, the press version of his love life is a lot more exciting than the reality. He worries what his parents will think if they pick up a paper and see his so-called romantic exploits in the headlines. He often tries to warn them, but he sometimes doesn't get to them fast enough. "My poor mom," he said. "She reads all this stuff about me and then she calls and asks if it's true."

The truth is Brad is very shy around women. He's the boy next door, a regular guy from Missouri who just happened to become a star. He's a thoroughly nice guy, the kind of boy a girl would bring home to Mother. His brother says Hollywood hasn't changed Brad one bit—he's the same as he always was: caring, charming and fiercely independent. Doug explained, "If the rush was for everyone to go out and buy Harleys, Brad wouldn't buy one."

Over the next few years, Brad definitely sees himself settling down. He looks forward to getting married and having kids. He was raised in such a close-knit family that he believes in the importance of sharing his life with someone and raising his own kids. Both his siblings, Doug and Julie, have children, and Uncle Brad adores them.

It must be hard for Brad to think about settling down right now because he's so busy with his acting. Being an actor takes him away on location for months at a time. At the moment he's enjoying his career. He knows there will come a time when his work will slow down and he can concentrate on becoming a family man. But while he's this hot, he's going to keep up the fast pace.

One reason Brad has dated actresses is because they understand his hectic work schedule. The only problem is that if two people are each working on their own careers, it may spell disaster for their relationship. Brad and Juliette Lewis were a case in point. With both their careers heating up, they found themselves away on location in different cities, and that put a strain on their relationship that contributed to their ultimate breakup.

Brad has come to the realization that his career is the only "significant other" in his life right now. He has found that juggling a career and a relationship is a lot like roller-skating uphill.

That's the reason why he sees different women, not getting serious just yet.

Since he has dated so many different women, the big question is: What kind of woman does Brad really go for? When asked what he looks for in a woman, he winced. "Ah, the dreaded question!" he said, grinning. "To tell you the truth, one minute I know what I want and then I find someone totally different. I *do* like someone with a sense of humor."

Brad confessed that he doesn't have a favorite "type" of woman. Instead he looks for "someone who is sincere, who likes to have a good time. I like to be with a woman who makes me laugh."

As for appearance, Brad likes a natural look. He isn't the type of guy who fusses with his clothes or hair. In fact, a woman who spends hours blow-drying her hair and getting ready for a date is a complete turnoff to Brad. He's spontaneous. He lives for the moment. He'll often do unpredictable things like jumping into his Cherokee and just driving. He needs to be with someone who is just as spontaneous.

What is Brad's idea of a perfect date? In his early years in California, when he had little money to spend, his favorite place to take a woman was to Shakey's for a $3.49 pizza. Now he likes to do a lot of different things, depending on his mood. He enjoys taking long walks on the beach and spending time alone, away from crowds. Other times he'll go to his favorite club, LunaPark. His friend actor Dermot Mulroney has a band called the Sweet & Low Orchestra that often plays at the club. Brad tries to maintain his friendship with Dermot and often pops into the club to listen to his new tunes.

Recently Brad dated actress Jitka Pohlodek, a dark-haired Czech whom he met at a party. They immediately hit it off; Brad even escorted Jitka to the premiere of *Legends of the Fall*. But they are just good friends now.

He's also been linked with Courtney Love, Kurt Cobain's widow and leader of the band Hole. Brad's reputed get-togethers with Courtney have generated some heat in the tabloids. Perhaps that's because of Courtney's reportedly wild lifestyle. But Brad and Courtney have never been anything more than just friends.

Brad has also been spotted around L.A. with Gwyneth Paltrow, who plays his love interest in the film *Seven*. Gwyneth is the daughter of actress Blythe Danner and Bruce Paltrow, and some say she and Brad seem very close. Did their onscreen romance continue once the cameras stopped rolling? It remains to be seen whether

Gwyneth will be the woman who takes Holly-wood's dreamiest bachelor out of circulation.

At least for now, Brad says he doesn't have a steady girlfriend. When it comes to the question of love and settling down, he said, ''Being in love is great, but I'm in no hurry to jump into anything serious right now. You'll have to get back to me on this subject in a couple of years.''

fourteen

Brad's Future

"I just want to play a guy who has a good time!"

That announcement from Brad Pitt came after it was reported he was to play a cop in his next movie, *Seven*. "I figured I'd give that a try," he said about the thriller. "This guy has no problems, that's the key thing. He's just a cop having fun and chasing the bad guy. It's been a blast to work on."

The set of *Seven* was basically a trouble-free environment for Brad. The only mishap occurred when Brad accidentally pushed his hand through a car windshield during a stunt. He needed several stitches, but a spokeswoman assured everyone that he was fine: "It was just a freak accident. He's back in the saddle again."

Seven is directed by David Fincher (*Alien 3*) and stars Morgan Freeman as Brad's partner.

The two cops are on the trail of a killer whose murders refer to the seven deadly sins. Brad really had a great time with that role. It gave him the chance to act in an entirely new genre. The only thing his loyal fans were upset about was that Brad had to cut his hair to play the role. But after his long, flowing locks were cut, Brad got used to his new cropped style.

Over the years Brad has changed his look numerous times. He likes to experiment with different hair lengths, and sometimes he goes days without shaving. For *Interview With the Vampire*, his hair was dyed brown, and when he was finished with it, he started to bleach it blond. His hairstylist, Thom Priano, said, "He likes long hair and the beard. It lets him show another side of himself."

The world got its first glimpse of Brad's new buzz-cut at the 1994 Golden Globe Awards, at which he was nominated for his performance in *Legends of the Fall*. It was his first nomination, and he considered it a great honor to be recognized for his portrayal of Tristan in *Legends*. The evening was a whirlwind of activity as photographers and reporters swarmed around Brad to ask how he felt about his success. He did his best to pose for photos while answering interviewers' questions.

Dealing with success from day to day can be a lot to handle for a down-to-earth guy like Brad. "This last year, I've been as happy as I've ever been, been miserable, been genius, been congratulated, been put down," he said. "The whole gamut of emotions."

Many things have changed for Brad, and he's just now learning to adjust. Since his back-to-back blockbusters came out, he's been inundated by a steady stream of scripts. It doesn't seem to matter that his asking price per movie has more than doubled, rising to $7 million. Brad is the hottest actor onscreen, and everyone in Hollywood wants to work with him. For the first time in his career, he can choose the roles he really wants to play.

In Hollywood tons of projects get discussed every day. Some find their way into film; most don't. When Brad worked with Ralph Bakshi on *Cool World,* the two got along so well that they decided to do a movie about Chet Baker, with Brad playing the tormented trumpeter. Unfortunately, like so many other projects, this idea stayed in the talking stages. Other movies, too, have fallen through for Brad.

There have been many parts Brad turned down because they didn't feel right. Right after filming *Legends of the Fall* and *Interview With the Vam-*

pire, he was offered the lead in the movie version of the novel *A Simple Plan* by Scott Smith. It's the story of a man who finds $4.4 million in a downed plane; the discovery leads to disaster. Brad read the book and loved it but found the subject matter too disturbing. After the emotional ride he had been on for nine months with *Legends* and *Interview,* he was in no shape to dive into another depressing story.

Another role he passed on was the crucial part of the deputy mayor in the Al Pacino movie *City Hall.* That role eventually went to John Cusack.

There seems very little that Brad hasn't already done as an actor. He has portrayed a broad range of characters, bringing a poetic vulnerability to all his roles, even the unattractive ones. He seems to know exactly what he wants, and he will most likely get it. "I'd like to have a Wilford Brimley career," he said. "Wilford's straight down the pipe. He's an actor who's been working his whole life who didn't become a star. That would be ideal. But who knows, it could all go away."

To keep his work interesting, Brad decided to take a role in the time-travel thriller *The Twelve Monkeys,* directed by Terry Gilliam. In this movie, which also stars Bruce Willis and Madeleine Stowe, Brad will play a character who has to fight off a virus that could destroy Earth. It's the kind of movie Brad would have loved watching when he was a kid; that was one reason he decided to do it.

What he's always looking for is the chance to do something different onscreen. "I choose films that have a flavor of whatever I'm feeling at the moment," he said.

Brad is the kind of guy who does things because he believes in them. He was the reader on the audio version of his favorite novel, *All the Pretty Horses* by Cormac McCarthy, and there is talk that it might be turned into a major movie. Brad has already expressed interest in playing the lead character, but that's down the road.

One movie that's reportedly in the planning stages is a sequel to *Interview With the Vampire*. Since the first film grossed more than $100 million, everyone involved is interested in bringing *The Vampire Lestat,* the second installment of Anne Rice's Vampire Chronicles series, to the big screen. Already signed up are Tom Cruise, Christian Slater, Antonio Banderas and director Neil Jordan.

Will Brad sharpen his fangs to play Louis again? He says it's a possibility because "Louis is only in the next book for about five minutes. He comes in and all the other vampires hate him because he squealed on them. They want to see him on a leash. That might be fun.''

As for his hair, which is so short now it would take a while to grow it out, Brad says, "I'm into the no-maintenance look. I don't even want to grow it out again to play Louis. I'd put on a wig.''

Brad Pitt has provided hours of magic moments to countless filmgoers around the world, and he has more surprises up his sleeve. He's come a long way from the heartland, and he has an even longer way to go.

He's built his entire career on taking chances, and there are plenty of roles he still wants to play. Whatever happens in the years ahead, there's no question that his career is on track.

So now that Brad knows he has achieved success as an actor, would he take the risk and do it all over again? Would he drop everything and drive west with nothing but a suitcase full of dreams in hopes of breaking into show business?

"Oh, yeah. Sure," he said, smiling. "I would do it all again. I think what everyone is looking for is something big. And when it happens, the happening is big. It's been a great ride! A very big ride!''

For hot and sexy Brad Pitt, that ride has taken him all the way to the top!

Brad's Vital Statistics

Full real name: William Bradley Pitt

Nickname: The Pittbull

Birthdate: December 18, 1963

Birthplace: Shawnee, Oklahoma

Height: 6 feet

Weight: 155 pounds

Hair color: dark blond

Eye color: blue

Brother and sister: Doug (nicknamed Digger) and Julie (nicknamed Jules)

Parents: Bill and Jane

First ambition: to be a race-car driver

First album bought: *Captain Fantastic* by Elton John

First crush: Farrah Fawcett. After seeing her on *Charlie's Angels,* Brad thought she was the prettiest woman on TV.

Favorite sports: mountain biking, waterskiing

Favorite movies: *Planet of the Apes, Ordinary People*

Favorite actors: Jack Nicholson, Mickey Rourke, Sean Penn

Favorite actresses: Debra Winger, Holly Hunter, Meg Ryan

Favorite architect: Charles Rennie Mackintosh

Favorite novel: *All the Pretty Horses* by Cormac McCarthy. Brad was the reader on the audio version of the book.

Favorite car: 1955 Thunderbird convertible

Favorite clothes: old jeans, worn leather

Favorite school subjects: journalism, art

Worst school subject: French

Little-known fact: Brad was voted Best Dressed in his high-school yearbook.

Musical instruments played: harmonica, guitar

Favorite childhood memory: summers at the lake

Favorite hobbies: art, writing, reading. "I like to take road trips with no destination and no time limits."

Professional ambition: "to be an incredible actor who makes people think."

What's on Brad's Mind?

ON HIMSELF
"I'm an insider looking out. Growing up, I was always an insider, inside of everything, like the cool stuff at school—but always looking *out*."

ON THE MONEY HE HAS EARNED
"I'm just getting the opportunity to make some decent money. Any money I've come into up to now I've put into land, so I'm pretty much broke."

ON COOKING
"That takes up too much time. I have a Snakmaster. You take two pieces of bread and whatever else you have in the house and throw it in and smash it down. I lived a whole summer on that."

ON ACTING
"I love to be able to do this—to run around and have adventures!"

ON *LEGENDS OF THE FALL*
"The movie is about sinking below, rising above, going off, giving up, taking charge, taking control. This man's journey seemed very accurate to me and very true."

On *Interview With the Vampire*
"Somewhere in the fourth week, I started responding to things differently, like my character would respond. I didn't like that."

On Stardom
"People have been asking me, 'What is it like to be a star?' I don't feel like a star. It's work—that's all it is."

On His Reasons for Playing Unusual Roles
"You take a movie because there's something it brings to you that you want to investigate. I felt like I'd done the serial-killer guy (in *Kalifornia*) and everything was going in that direction. And I wanted to go to a place where somebody cared about something."

On His Future
"There are a million things to be and do. You just have to get out and do them. People get too concerned about money. People limit themselves too much. I have a million things I want to do."

Filmography

LESS THAN ZERO (1987)
Brad was an extra.

CUTTING CLASS (1989)
Directed by: Rospo Pallenberg
Produced by: Rudy Cohen and Donald R. Beck
Screenplay by: Steve Slavkin
Music by: Jill Fraser
Released by: Gower Street

Brian Woods	Donovan Leitch
Paula Carson	Jill Schoelen
Dwight Ingalls	Brad Pitt
Mr. Dante	Roddy McDowall
William Carson III	Martin Mull
Coach Harris	Dirk Blocker

HAPPY TOGETHER (1990)
Directed by: Mel Damski
Produced by: Jere Henshaw
Screenplay by: Craig J. Nevius
Music by: Robert Folk
Released by: Seymour Borde

Christopher Wooden	Patrick Dempsey
Alexandra Page	Helen Slater
Gooseflesh	Dan Schneider

Slash	Kevin Hardesty
Ruth Carpenter	Barbara Babcock
Luisa Dellacova	Gloria Hayes
Brian	Brad Pitt

ACROSS THE TRACKS (1991)
Directed by: Sandy Tung
Produced by: Dale Rosenbloom
Screenplay by: Sandy Tung
Music by: Joel Goldsmith
Released by: Desert Productions

Billy Maloney	Rick Schroder
Joe Maloney	Brad Pitt
Louie	David Anthony Marshall
Rosemary Maloney	Carrie Snodgress

THELMA & LOUISE (1991)
Directed by: Ridley Scott
Produced by: Ridley Scott, Mimi Polk
Coproduced by: Dean O'Brien, Callie Khouri
Screenplay by: Callie Khouri
Director of Photography: Adrian Biddle
Edited by: Thom Noble
Music by: Hans Zimmer
Released by: MGM/Pathé

Thelma	Geena Davis
Louise	Susan Sarandon
Hal	Harvey Keitel

Jimmy	Michael Madsen
Darryl	Christopher McDonald
Max	Stephen Tobolowsky
J.D.	Brad Pitt
Harlan	Timothy Carhart

JOHNNY SUEDE (1992)

Directed by: Tom DiCillo
Produced by: Ruth Waldburger, Yoram Mandel
Screenplay by: Tom DiCillo
Director of Photography: Joe DeSalvo
Edited by: Geraldine Peroni
Music by: Jim Farmer
Released by: Miramax

Johnny Suede	Brad Pitt
Darlette	Alison Moir
Winston	Ron Vawter
Dalton	Dennis Parlato
Mrs. Fontaine	Tina Louise
Yvonne	Catherine Keener

COOL WORLD (1992)

Directed by: Ralph Bakshi
Produced by: Frank Mancuso, Jr.
Screenplay by: Mark Victor, Michael Grais, Larry Gross
From a story by: Ralph Bakshi, Frank Mancuso, Jr.

Director of Photography: John A. Alonzo
Edited by: Steve Mirkovich, Annamaria Szanto
Music by: Mark Isham
Released by: Paramount Pictures

Jack Deebs	Gabriel Byrne
Holli Would	Kim Basinger
Frank Harris	Brad Pitt
Mom Harris	Janni Brenn-Lowen
Comic-Book Store Cashier	Carrie Hamilton

Voices of: Frank Sinatra, Jr., Jenine Jennings, Gregory Snegoff, Candy Milo, Joey Camen

A RIVER RUNS THROUGH IT (1992)
Directed by: Robert Redford
Produced by: Robert Redford, Patrick Markey
Screenplay by: Richard Friedenberg
From the novella by: Norman Maclean
Director of Photography: Philippe Rousselot
Edited by: Lynzee Klingman, Robert Estrin
Music by: Mark Isham
Released by: Columbia Pictures

Paul Maclean	Brad Pitt
Norman Maclean	Craig Sheffer
Reverend Maclean	Tom Skerritt
Mrs. Maclean	Brenda Blethyn
Jesse Burns	Emily Lloyd
Mrs. Burns	Edie McClurg
Narration	Robert Redford

KALIFORNIA (1993)

Directed by: Dominic Sena
Produced by: Steve Golin, Sigurjon Sighvatsson, Aristides McGarry
Screenplay by: Tim Metcalfe
Director of Photography: Bojan Bazelli
Edited by: Martin Hunter
Music by: Carter Burwell
Released by: Gramercy Pictures

Early Grayce	Brad Pitt
Adele Corners	Juliette Lewis
Brian Kessler	David Duchovny
Carrie Laughlin	Michelle Forbes
Walter Livesay	Gregory Mars Martin

TRUE ROMANCE (1993)

Directed by: Tony Scott
Produced by: Samuel Hadida, Steve Perry, Bill Unger
Screenplay by: Quentin Tarantino
Director of Photography: Jeffrey L. Kimball, A.S.C.
Music by: Hans Zimmer
Released by: Warner Brothers

Clarence Worley	Christian Slater
Alabama Whitman	Patricia Arquette
Clifford Worley	Dennis Hopper
Mentor	Val Kilmer

Drexl Spivey	Gary Oldman
Floyd (Dick's Roommate)	Brad Pitt
Vincenzo Coccotti	Christopher Walken
Big Don	Samuel L. Jackson

THE FAVOR (1994)
Directed by: Donald Petrie
Produced by: Lauren Shuler-Donner
Screenplay by: Sara Parriott, Josann McGibbon
Director of Photography: Tim Suhrstedt
Music by: Thomas Newman
Released by: Orion Pictures

Kathy	Harley Jane Kozak
Emily	Elizabeth McGovern
Peter	Bill Pullman
Elliott	Brad Pitt
Joe Dubin	Larry Miller
Tom Andrews	Ken Wahl

INTERVIEW WITH THE VAMPIRE (1994)
Directed by: Neil Jordan
Produced by: David Geffen, Stephen Woolley
Screenplay by: Anne Rice, based on her novel
Director of Photography: Philippe Rousselot,
    A.F.C.
Music by: Elliot Goldenthal
Vampire makeup and effects by: Stan Winston
Released by: Warner Brothers

Louis De Ponte Du Lac	Brad Pitt
Malloy the Interviewer	Christian Slater
Lestat	Tom Cruise
Claudia	Kirsten Dunst
Santiago	Stephen Rea
Armand	Antonio Banderas

LEGENDS OF THE FALL (1994)

Directed by: Edward Zwick

Produced by: Edward Zwick, Bill Witliff, Marshall Herskovitz

Screenplay by: Susan Shilliday, Bill Wittliff

Based on the novella by: Jim Harrison

Director of Photography: John Toll

Music by: James Horner

Released by: TriStar Pictures

Tristan Ludlow	Brad Pitt
William Ludlow	Anthony Hopkins
Alfred Ludlow	Aidan Quinn
Susannah	Julia Ormond
Samuel Ludlow	Henry Thomas
Isabel Two	Karina Lombard
One Stab	Gordon Tootoosis

SEVEN (1995)

Directed by: David Fincher

Released by: New Line Cinema

Starring: Brad Pitt, Morgan Freeman, Gwyneth
   Paltrow

THE TWELVE MONKEYS (1995)
Directed by: Terry Gilliam
Released by: Universal Pictures
Starring: Brad Pitt, Bruce Willis, Madeleine
   Stowe

TELEVISION APPEARANCES
Commercials for Levi's jeans and Mountain Dew
   soda
Another World (daytime drama)
Dallas (Brad played Randy in five episodes.)
Growing Pains (guest appearance)
21 Jump Street (guest appearance)
Head of the Class (guest appearance)
Trial and Error (guest appearance)
Thirtysomething (guest appearance)
Tales from the Crypt (guest appearance)
Glory Days (Series. Brad played Walker Love-
   joy.)
The Image (HBO movie)
Too Young to Die? (TV movie. Brad played Billy.)

ABOUT THE AUTHOR

Grace Catalano is the author of two *New York Times* best-sellers: *New Kids on the Block* and *New Kids on the Block Scrapbook*. Her other books include biographies of Joey Lawrence, Jason Priestly, Paula Abdul, Gloria Estefan, Richard Grieco, Fred Savage, River Phoenix, Alyssa Milano and Kirk Cameron. She is also the author of *Teen Star Yearbook,* which includes minibiographies of eighty-five celebrities. Grace Catalano has edited numerous magazines, including *Rock Legend, Star Legend, The Movie Times, CountryBeat, Country Style* and the teen magazine *Dream Guys*. She and her brother, Joseph, wrote and designed *Elvis: A Tenth Anniversary Tribute, Elvis and Priscilla* and *Country Music's Hottest Stars*. Grace Catalano lives on the North Shore of Long Island.